A COMPLICATED GRACE

A collaborative memoir of addiction, grief, and forgiveness

By Dave Hillis

Published by

⽼BitterSweetBooks

ISBN 978-1-958865-04-0

This publication also includes works from the public domain:

'Diary of an Old Soul' by George MacDonald

'Emancipation' by Emily Dickinson

'He Told Me a Joke' by Meister Eckhart

'I am Much Too Alone in This World, Yet Not Alone Enough' by Rainer Maria Rilke

'If–' by Rudyard Kipling

'If Someone Cried in Heaven' by Catherine of Siena

'Invictus' by William Ernest Henley

'Last Night As I Was Sleeping' by Antonio Machado

'Sonnet 116' by William Shakespeare

'Sitting by a Bush in Broad Sunlight' by Robert Frost

'Stopping by Woods on a Snowy Evening' by Robert Frost

'The Merchant of Venice' by William Shakespeare

'The Need to Win' by Chuang Tzu

'The Road Not Taken' by Robert Frost

'The Second Coming' by William Butler Yeats

Editing by Kate Schmidgall and Avery Marks
Cover design and creative direction by Obiekwe "Obi" Okolo
Typesetting by Greg Sitzmann
Photography by Scott Lewis
Production and operations by Dave Baker

Praise for *A Complicated Grace*

This book—transparent and unaffected, raw and *real*—is laced with hope and heartache, poetry and faith, warmth and wounds. *A Complicated Grace* is about a complicated soul, a beautiful soul, a child of God, told by those who knew him best and loved him most. Through their words they have turned Jordan's life and memory into a gift they have generously shared with the rest of us.

–Peter Wehner, Contributing writer, *The New York Times*, Contributing writer, *The Atlantic*, Senior Fellow at The Trinity Forum

"*A Complicated Grace*, in addition to being a remarkable tribute to local love, to family and friends, reaches out to offer succour to anyone who trembles on the brink of tilling the unturned soil of memories not yet detoxified. To show there is a whole-making through losses yet-to-be understood. For not only is grace complicated: it is true, and it trues us."

–James Alison, Catholic theologian, priest, author of *Jesus the Forgiving Victim*

"Searing, challenging, riveting, inspiring, and real."

–Father James Martin, S.J., author of *Learning to Pray*

"Dave Hillis is a leader with great depth and wisdom. His reflections are certain to bless many who encounter the 'complicated grace' of their own lives."

–Curtis Chang, Executive Director of Redeeming Babel, host of The Good Faith Podcast, author of *The Anxiety Opportunity*

"*A Complicated Grace* is a complicated gift, which at once anguishes the heart and captivates the soul. Dave Hillis, with both vulnerability and courage, invites us into an intimate reflection on the mysteries of love, loss, suffering, and hope. It is a story of the tenacious love of a father for his son, told with breathtaking poetic and theological insight, casting light and consolation for all who know the complexity of addiction and grief."

–Kerry Alys Robinson, President and CEO of Catholic Charities USA, author of *Imagining Abundance*

"If any of the 150 Psalms speak to your heart, *A Complicated Grace* will do so as well. Be prepared to experience a profound range of emotions as letters, poems, and reflections illuminate the life and death of Jordan Hillis. This son, father, brother, uncle, and friend lived deeply and died tragically. His struggles, failures, loves, and gifts live on in these writings, drawing us into his life, and perhaps, our own. If you are a parent, grandparent, child, or, have loved and lost, you will find grace, in all its complications, in these pages."

–Daryl Grigsby, author of *Catholics for the Common Good*

"A book whose form gently incarnates the most personal mysteries of light and shadow, *A Complicated Grace* comes as that rarest of friends—one willing to accompany our wrestling with God. For all those who have uttered the cry of love to a child and feared it would go unheard, this book is for you."

–Anne Snyder, Editor-in-Chief of Comment magazine, host of "The Whole Person Revolution" podcast, author of *The Fabric of Character*

"*A Complicated Grace* is a deeply tender, break-your-heart-beautiful memoir of a father's love for his gifted and troubled son. It shows the power of poetry to penetrate even the confines of prison with beauty and hope, and the potency of love in beholding one's beloved amidst life's messiness. And above all, it is a story of grace that permeates grief, heartbreak, and loss. For anyone struggling with the costs and complications of love: you will want to read this book."

–Cherie Harder, President of The Trinity Forum

"The Hebrew word for *mercy* means womb-space. That's what mercy does: It calls forth life. The reflections in *A Complicated Grace* are the womb-space of a grief-stricken and broken-hearted community in the wake of unbearable loss. It is a space that holds a certain kind of untamable and big hearted realness that mirrors the life and loss of the one that inspires these reflections. It's almost too much to take in all at once. My suggestion is to go slow. And perhaps, like me, you'll discover yourself being made alive in the presence of mercy itself—the kind that imperceptibly infiltrates the tiniest crack of our granite like grief, like a vein of grace, infusing us with life… from within."

–Kris Rocke, CEO of Street Psalms, co-author of Geography of Grace

"*A Complicated Grace* is a heartfelt offering for those who grieve. Through letters to his late son, interwoven with poignant poetry, Hillis captures the complex chords of faith, vulnerability, loss, and hope. As a grieving mother who has also lost a child, this memoir resonated deeply, reflecting both my personal grief and our shared sorrow for those lost loved ones. It does more than merely touch on the familiar themes of loss; it dives into the deeper harmonics that sustain us through grief when simple platitudes fall short. Humanizing, hopeful, and profoundly real."

–Chelsea Langston Bombino, Program Officer of Fetzer Institute

"*A Complicated Grace* captures how many different truths can coexist together. Through letters and thought provoking poems, Hillis shares with vulnerable authenticity about parenting, faith, and love as it enters and lives in unclear paths that eventually lead to the unimaginable. This story, deeply felt by the reader, is a testament to the complicated grace that life can be—beautiful and heartbreaking, simple and unfathomable, all at once."

–Julie Lewis, Founder of The 30/30 Project, co-author of Still Positive

"One 'vein' of grace in my life is to know the Hillis Family. *A Complicated Grace* is of enormous help to all of us who struggle with the uncertainties that surround every "village" that raises a child. Jordan would be pleased."

–Rev. Dr. Larry Lloyd, President of Leadership Foundations,
author of Recovering from Racism

"*A Complicated Grace* beautifully witnesses to what redemptive love in action looks and feels like. It tells the quintessential Christian story: the unfailing love of a father for his son becomes manifest in the world, not in spite of life's challenges but because of them. If ever you doubt what incarnational love looks like, spend some time meditating with Dave and Jordan."

–Daniel Cardinali, Board Chair, The Fetzer Institute

"*A Complicated Grace* touched me deeply; it made me think, and it made me pray. It's a learned, eloquent, deeply thoughtful book; sometimes searing, often beautiful, and achingly authentic."

–Chris Lowney, author of *Make Today Matter*

"*A Complicated Grace* invites you into the most delicate and intimate of exchanges—the expressions of love and encouragement between a parent and a child, both yearning to be there for the other as best they can in times of difficulty. Hillis has woven together a beautiful testimony to his son, his family, and his community, interspersing his own writing with some of the most moving, grace-filled poems of our day. For families who love someone who is struggling, or who deeply miss someone whose struggle is behind them, *A Complicated Grace* will feel at once familiar and a refreshingly candid act of accompaniment."

–Leslie MacKrell, Partner of The Bridgespan Group

"Dave's eloquence, his profound faith, and his own spiritual journey are reflected in the beauty and poignancy of these poems and letters to his beloved son. This book touched me deeply with the yearning of a father for his son and with the sense of hope and renewal captured in these passages. *A Complicated Grace* is a blessing to all who are seeking hope and encouragement in the midst of loss and grief, as well as those of us navigating our own paths into faith and grace."

–Bill Milliken, Founder of Communities In Schools, author of *The Last Dropout*

"One of the keys to a good memoir is whether the author's voice surfaces in transparent and authentic ways. *A Complicated Grace* rises to the occasion. It is a book where the author leads with a heart that is simultaneously broken and hope-filled. The book is poetic beyond its rich poetry. It is not only a luminous reflection, but also a light for all those who have been darkened by grief and graced with moments of joy."

–Dr. William P. Robinson, President Emeritus of Whitworth University, author of *Incarnate Leadership*

Dedication

It was quite clear from the beginning who *A Complicated Grace* should be dedicated to. Jordan Michael Hillis—Daddy, Uncle Jo, Uncle Jordan, Jo—always had six particular young people top of mind. It is to you that this memoir is dedicated with the hopes and prayers that Jordan, as a part of the community of saints, will pray that you will experience what St. Paul described in Ephesians:

> *That Christ may dwell in your hearts through faith; that you, being rooted and grounded in love, may be able to comprehend with all the saints what is the width and length and depth and height—to know the love of Christ which passes knowledge; that you may be filled with all the fullness of God.*[1]

To his beloved children, Jimmy David (JD) and Londyn (Londy) Capri, who he could not have loved more. Name the metaphor—the wind at his back, a pine tree growing on a granite rock, the wind beneath his wings—you two were all of those and many more for him. There was simply nothing that came close to the joy he experienced in your presence. And while both of you do not fully realize it now, it is my prayer that this memoir will be an everlasting reminder of how he loved and cherished you and, perhaps just as importantly, that he was and is loved and cherished by many.

And to the cousins of JD and Londy: If it is possible that an

---

1 Ephesians 3:17-19, NKJV

uncle could love a nephew and nieces any more deeply than Uncle Jo loved you, Kenedee Ryan, Myles Patrick, Jae Lynn and Fiona Maeve, I have not witnessed it. To say that Jordan viewed you as his own would be a gross understatement. He took as much delight in your flourishing as he did in the blossoming of JD and Londy. Cousins, as Jordan understood, were of a special species in that they represented what was both given to you by way of birth and what you also got to choose—the rarest of combinations.

Finally, it is important to note that Jordan prayed for all of you often. One of those prayers was tattooed on his body: "Let the real you, see the real me, holding nothing back." Let it be so for the six of you and know that you now have Daddy/Uncle Jo in heaven cheering you on.

August 1, 2024,
Mount Angel Benedictine Abbey, Saint Benedict, Oregon

Letters, Poems & Mishpacha Reflections

Foreword
By Father Steve Lantry, S.J.

There is a paradox at the heart of every human. While the outlines differ from person to person, the essential elements are similar. We all have some gifts—recognized or not—and of course we all have our deficits. Some experiences enlarge our growth, making us more human. Still other experiences diminish us, making us less human. The crux of the paradox seems to be that, whatever our greatest gift might be, it can sometimes turn into our greatest weakness.

I believe this to be true of Jordan Hillis. In certain ways he was a classic study of opposites. In conventional educational settings he struggled with a learning disability; yet he was highly intelligent. In large part because of his experience of the streets, he was very perceptive about other people—good at "reading" others. And he was very intuitive in social situations— he didn't miss much. He also seemed to have extra-ordinary spiritual sensitivity.

Jordan certainly experienced trauma in his life, the kind that leaves scars and becomes part of whatever permanent burden one carries. In response to the difficulties through which he passed, Jordan developed considerable inner strength, expressed not least in a powerful will. Many who knew him have noted his total commitment to any endeavor he undertook. Moreover, that same will to commitment expressed itself in an unwavering loyalty to family and friends. He was a fierce friend.

Thanks to the friendship between me and Jordan's father, Dave,

I was around Jordan socially a great deal over many years. My lasting memory of the quality of his presence is one of deep goodness; he was a person holding deep compassion for others. Having needed and received kindness himself, he was remarkably kind to others. The biblical term for this is *merciful*. Generally, his judgments of others were right.

Before I speak about his most serious manifestation of the human paradox mentioned above, let me make my own confession. I am quite sure that I am not alone in having regrets in the aftermath of Jordan's death. When he was suffering with the worst of his addiction, Dave asked me to call Jordan. When I did, he answered, but before we could talk there was a knock at his door and he said he'd call me the next day. When he didn't, I felt I should have called again, *but I didn't*. Much later, at the end of a visit with Dave and Teresa, as I left the house, I saw Jordan with a close friend talking on the west patio. I got in the car and thought that I should go and say goodbye, *but I didn't*, my reason being I didn't want to interrupt. Needless to say, I wish I had done so.

Like most people, I have struggled with addiction and I have my own experience of what is called "incomprehensible demoralization." One of the most essential elements in recovery, perhaps the most essential, is the need for surrender to what is called *a power greater than ourselves*. Surrender is essential because in the throes of addiction, the will is completely undermined—will power is literally useless. But of course an addicted person is incapable of perceiving this. This failure of will produces an intense and constant sense of shame, something that can never be shared with another person.

This seems to me to be the paradox of Jordan's final months. And even though he was being helped toward finding the power he needed, his always powerful will became his greatest obstacle. As Dr. Gerald May says in his excellent book, *Addiction and Grace*, addiction "distorts reality,"[2] and so our perception, no matter how finely tuned, not only doesn't help, it hinders. He says further, "My self-esteem crumbles as I sense how truly out of control I am. I am in the clutches of the enemy, and the enemy is myself."[3]

Because addiction creates a terrible inner isolation we are cut off from the surest flow of grace, namely, community. Part of the tragedy of Jordan's final days is that, even though his family were able to pierce his denial enough for him to agree to go to treatment, his distorted thought was to go on his own terms. This led directly to his untimely death. Jordan's exceptional gift was his will to commit, whether activities or persons. But his will, distorted by addiction, was his undoing.

Often when relating the details of some difficulty—usually a relationship—when asked for clarity we will say, "It's complicated." We don't mean that we can't understand the situation at all, we just can't explain why things are the way they are. From the outside, other people's difficulties and their solutions may seem obvious to us. But we know from our own complicated experiences that there is nothing obvious at all about how to resolve what is most difficult. We experience a powerlessness in the face of such persistent human conundrums,

2 Dr. Gerald May, M.D. *Addiction and Grace* (Harper & Row, Inc., 1988), 50.
3 May, *Addiction and Grace*, 60.

so it's no surprise how much more powerless we feel in the presence of someone else's complicated struggle.

It is my experience of Jordan, and my reflection in the aftermath of his seemingly inexplicable death, that produced the phrase, "a complicated grace." And even though I have written in a way that suggests his life and death all make sense to me, that is not the case at all. His death in particular still seems so unnecessary, so unfair.

I am willing to turn my own will and judgment over to that power, however we understand it, which seeks only our good. As the theologian James Alison has said of this power, "…God holds our shame tenderly."[4] It is that tenderness that we all desire that now holds Jordan in a way which we who remain can only imagine. It seems to me completely reasonable that I would pray, not for Jordan, but to him for the kind of help we all need.

---

4 James Alison, "Catholicity, Shame, and Polarization," Candlemas Lecture, Boston College, February 7, 2024.

Preface

The oft quoted African proverb is certainly true: it does take a village. It takes the magical alchemy of mothers and fathers, aunties and uncs, grandfathers and grandmothers, siblings and cousins, coaches and teachers, neighbors and friends to rally around a young person for any possibility of future flourishing. To try, as best as they can, to offer different forms of ballast to steady through the stormy waters of growing up. We mark these years of harrowing navigation with moments of celebration: birthday parties, graduation ceremonies, religious rites of passage, weddings. Woven together, these rites and rituals become the backdrop for the village's collective and conscious celebration of the child—representations of our best selves and best efforts.

But how does a village grieve the loss of a child?

Where does one turn with others when the heart is shattered, emotions shredded; when the unspeakable thing that you feared would happen does? How do people within the village look to each other without casting blame, scapegoating, or acting as victims?

More difficult still, where does one turn when the village itself might be culpable for the loss of the child? Where does one place the regret of the unanswered phone call because of your sense of despair? How does one sit with the car ride or errand you didn't offer because you found yourself to be too tired and worn down? What do you do with the prayer life that became increasingly muted because you didn't believe God was going to do anything anyway? How do you process the sense of resignation that hurtled toward resentment because for this particular child to succeed given what he was born with would require a Hail Mary pass; or the guilt over the opportunities that surfaced, but you didn't have either the resource or the resolve to make it happen? How does one unsee the face of tears and the voice of despair knowing there was nothing that you could do to assuage the grief of another failed school assignment; or the guttural screams of the trauma felt after another written driving test was flunked? Where to turn when we saw the look of crushing shame when, as early as preschool, we knew school was not going to be a place of comfort and care? The literature and resources needed for the village to walk through these and other questions is pretty thin.

As a result, the village will often do one of three things. It flees—looking for a place in which it can benignly hide itself. It fights—running toward the child with a frenetic energy that often inflicts more violence. It freezes—becoming powerless to do anything for fear that they might make the situation worse. We know all too well that it is one thing to quote Emerson and believe "that everything God makes has a crack in it"[5] and quite another thing to live together with those cracks showing up in unseemly, uncontrollable and, perhaps most destructive of all, in unhopeful ways.

This memoir is for those countless individuals who make up 'the village'—those who pledged and committed, by way of

---

5 Ralph Waldo Emerson, "Compensation." in *The Essays of Ralph Waldo Emerson*, ed. Alfred R. Ferguson and Jean F. Carr (Cambridge: Belknap Press, 1987), 49.

bloodline or social connection, to a child's flourishing and, for reasons only they know, feel like they failed. For those who followed every jot and tittle of whatever plan was being offered by the latest group focusing on the family to ensure your child would become light for this world and instead they lit up the world. It is for those who looked in the proverbial toolbox and found no tool for what they confronted. It is for those who knew, right from the beginning, that they did not embody the correct temperament, talent, and toughness to engage this particular child. It is for those who lived in proximity to the village down the street—the one that seemed to push all the right buttons and pull all the needed levers for their child's flourishing while yours withered on the vine. It is for those who, if they were either allowed or gave themselves permission to do so, would emit Whitman's "barbaric yawp"[6] of such epic portions that it would silence all those around them because, in the end, it wasn't you or others that failed. Not really. The pain of it all was that it was God who failed.

The poet Christian Wiman wrote: "Memory's mercies mostly aren't. But there are days, I swear, that are veined with grace."[7] What follows is an attempt to provide some language and reflection on the "memories" of a village raising a child that failed and where it often felt like they "mostly weren't." That child—my child—Jordan Michael Hillis died in my arms at 4:35 p.m. with his older brother looking on in the parking lot of a restaurant 10 minutes away from the drug rehab facility he

---

6 Walt Whitman, "Song of Myself, 52," in Academy of American Poets https://poets.org/poem/song-myself-52.

7 Christian Wiman, "Memory's Mercy," in *Once in the West: Poems* (NY: Farrar, Straus and Giroux, 2015), 41.

was to be admitted into within the hour. He lived for 38 years where "memory's mercies mostly weren't." It is our collective suspicion that there are many, perhaps thousands of villages who have a similar story. That when push comes to shove, if you were asked whether you and your village succeeded in raising your child in the ways you had first planned you would answer that we failed.

And yet. When one pauses to look into these "memory's mercies that mostly aren't" one can see places of "veined grace" in our failed child. They are "veined" in the sense that they are often hard to see or, for that matter, even recognize, but they are there. "I swear."

It is Jordan in the midst of his last week of life, drug drenched and visibly violent, still having the wherewithal to text his cousins and brothers to tell them how much he loved them and that they should be in better touch. It is Jordan, who had to be sequestered in our bedroom for fear that he would overdose, sitting on our deck with his head gently leaning on his girlfriend's shoulder. It is Jordan, who took every shit job that was ever given to him and became their best employee. It is Jordan, who with very little education became a wonderful poet and voluminous reader. It is Jordan, who through his experiences on the street and in prison became best-of-friends with an 80-year-old Jesuit priest. In the end, while this volume will as soberly, steadily, and solemnly state the complexity of being a part of Jordan's village, it will also lift up and cautiously, collectively, cheer for those "veins of grace" with the hope that you too will be strengthened in your spirit, resolute in your regard, and animated in your aspirations. That you can also see that we are all, in the end, a complicated grace.

How to Read This Book

This book is meant to be read slowly. Through this collection of letters, poems, and reflections, you will be carried along a journey of addiction, incarceration, forgiveness, grief, grace, and gratitude. It's our hope that you will find this book a helpful and hopeful companion as you navigate your own times of struggle.

Between 2010 - 2011 Jordan served time for drug-related crimes. During his incarceration Jordan's father Dave wrote him a letter each week—every Friday for 15 months. What follows is a collection of letters from a father to his son, interspersed with essays from the community that loved him.

We invite you to companion with the Hillis village, to walk slowly and consider the rhythms of pain and loss, mercy and hope, joy and celebration that they have so generously gifted.

We invite you, as Mary Oliver wrote, to linger and admire the things of this world that are kind, and maybe also troubled.

SPRING

Dear Jordan,   APRIL 9, 2010

Well here is the first of what will be many notes and letters I am planning on sending you every Friday while this process around you lasts. I hope you don't get bored with my thoughts, ideas, pieces of poetry, and ramblings about life. It will help me feel connected to you.

The gist of this note is to try and describe how very proud I am of you for the way you are taking care of business. Situations— whether personal, business, athletics, etc.—always hold within them possibilities. In effect, you can either choose to become a victim and bitter or you can be a victor and gracious. I think this is what Robert Frost meant when he wrote "two roads diverged in a wood and I—I took the one less traveled by, and that has made all the difference."[8]

I have for many years tried to decipher why some people choose one "road" versus the other and, at this point, I have no answers. What I can tell you is some of the signs of having taken that less traveled road.

The first and foremost sign is the transparency of the soul. I think (if I remember correctly) that your wonderful tattoo states exactly what transparency of the soul means when it says, "The real you holding nothing back." You have done a tremendous job of being transparent in this process and admitting to who you are and what you have done.

---

8 Robert Frost. 2021. "The Road Not Taken." in *Robert Frost Early Poetry Collection, 1913-1924: A Boy's Will, North of Boston, Mountain Interval, New Hampshire: a Poem with Notes and Grace Notes*, 95. N.p.: Independently Published.

The second sign is one of forgiveness, where you are able to both forgive yourself and ask for forgiveness of others. This, as you well know, is no easy task. It requires humility, which is one of the rarest traits I know. Once again, you have done a very good job of asking others for forgiveness. Thank you for that. I greatly admire your courage. On the other hand, I know that forgiving yourself is difficult. I pray that you will be overwhelmed with the grace of God and know, in your heart, that in Christ Jesus there is no condemnation.[9]

So my young brother... it is all good. I have already become a better person for the way you are handling things. Truth be told, you challenge me to be a bigger and better person.

With deep love and respect,

D

---

9 Romans 8:31-39

Jordan,

I hope you are well, my young brother. You have had quite a week. I continue to pray for you as often as I am prompted (and it seems I am prompted quite a bit) in hopes that my, along with others', prayers are of some kind of help and support to you.

With the news (and I think good… do you?) of the decision the court made, I am sure your mind is beginning to prepare for the next leg of your journey. And as you always do (given your chess playing sensibilities), I am sure you have thought through your next few moves. I am very confident that you will be fully prepared.

Speaking of the journey, did you receive the book I recommended (*Let the Great World Spin* by Colum McCann)? I want you to know that when I read the book a few weeks ago and encountered the character of Corrigan I instantly thought about you. I fell in love with his character because he reminded me so much of you. It seems to me you two are very similar in both your commitments and outlook. For example:

> *What Corrigan wanted was a fully believable God, one you could find in the grime of the everyday. The comfort he got from the hard, cold truth—the filth, the war, the poverty—was that life could be capable of small beauties. He wasn't interested in the glorious tales of the afterlife or the notions of a honey-soaked heaven. To him that was a dressing room for hell. Rather he consoled himself with the fact that, in the real world, when he looked closely*

into the darkness he might find the presence of a light, damaged and bruised, but a little light all the same.[10]

Do you agree with my assessment? It has always seemed to me that what you have been after in your journey is "a fully believable God" that when you "looked closely into the darkness" you "might find the presence of a light, damaged and bruised, but a little light all the same." I know you have given this gift to me. You have, in so many ways, forced me to examine and reexamine what I believe about God and to look for this God in both the dark places of this world and my life.

It seems to me that at least this is a part of the journey you are on—finding a "fully believable God." I have no doubt that when you do, you will commit to this God just like you have committed yourself to your friends, family, and so many other things.

I look forward to seeing you on Tuesday. I am bringing your boy Osterhaus with me who is also looking forward to seeing you.

I love you and have your back,

Dad

---

10 Colum McCann, *Let the Great World Spin* (NY: Random House, 2008), 20.

Jordan,

I hope you are well. I have been thinking and praying for you as I have imagined you in your new surroundings. My thinking and praying has also been fueled by the fact that I have decided to give up tobacco while you are away. It seemed to me that if you can show the kind of strength that you have, I should be in it with you.

I have been thinking a lot about you through a poem by Mary Oliver called "A Dream of Trees." I have enclosed the poem for you. There are a couple of lines that you, as much as anybody, have demonstrated to me.

The first is "Meanwhile I bend my heart toward lamentation," which I take to mean that if our involvement with each other is to be authentic it will have "lamentation" woven into it. This is one of the things I have always appreciated about you: your absolute courage to look at hard, sad, and uncomfortable realities and "bend your heart toward" them.

The second is the phrase: "Who ever made music of a mild day?" While some of your attempts—friends, struggle with authority, speaking your mind, etc.—have taken my breath away, I have never wondered if you were in a position to "make some music" because of your experiences. And while I know this latest experience has been and will be very difficult in some ways, I am also deeply confident that it will become the stuff that you are going to "make some music" out of in ways that bless a lot of people.

So thanks, Jo, for challenging me to "bend my heart toward lamentation" and "make music" out of my life. Interestingly, this poem was what helped me finally decide to take this job I am currently doing with Leadership Foundations.

Finally, I am hoping I can see you very soon. While I am glad that you are out of T-Town, I do miss the idea of how close you were when you were in the city jail. Here's to hoping I will see you shortly.

Your boy, D

A Dream of Trees
By Mary Oliver

There is a thing in me that dreamed of trees,
A quiet house, some green and modest acres
A little way from every troubling town,
A little way from factories, schools, laments.
I would have time, I thought, and time to spare,
With only streams and birds for company,
To build out of my life a few wild stanzas.
And then it came to me, that so was death,
A little way away from everywhere.

There is a thing in me still dreams of trees.
But let it go. Homesick for moderation,
Half the world's artists shrink or fall away.
If any find solution, let him tell it.
Meanwhile I bend my heart toward lamentation
Where, as the times implore our true involvement,
The blades of every crisis point the way.

I would it were not so, but so it is.
Who ever made music of a mild day?

MISHPACHA REFLECTIONS
County
By Ryan Hillis, Brother

My brother always seemed destined for some long, cold nights in the penitentiary. You could have foreseen it statistically, considering it wasn't until 4th grade that his dyslexia was finally discovered. Then, like any kid would, he picked up a book that interested him. Most kids his age would have gone for sports, fiction, or comics. But not J-O. He found himself drawn to organized crime, viewing figures like Whitey Bulger, Al Capone, Bumpy Johnson, and Frank Lucas as akin to Michael Jordan. One tattoo my brother later inked onto his body encapsulated his devotion to this lifestyle: *Omertà*, the code of silence, a mantra that holds for many until one gets caught by the authorities. As Jo's older brother, I can attest to the countless times I've benefited from this code, both within our household and occasionally out on the streets.

Understanding my brother required authenticity; he couldn't stand anything he perceived as fake. This sentiment was encapsulated in his tattoo, an acrostic-style poem: "Let The Real You, See The Real Me, Holding Nothing Back." When the day of his arrest arrived, it felt inevitable, like the rain in Tacoma. Though I am no expert on jail or prison life, I know that incarceration lays bare your true self; there's no hiding from it.

The call from my mom on that spring afternoon didn't surprise me. I was on my way home from Tacoma's Eastside when my phone buzzed. "Goddamn," I muttered as I absorbed the news. My mind raced, pondering which crime he might have been caught for. In all honesty, he caught a sweet deal. My brother was to spend the next 22 months behind bars. My role as his brother would have to shift from everyday moments spent together to prison phone calls and weekly visits to America's hell holes.

Jordan's time began as all prison sentences do, in county jail. My dad and I were the first to visit. The moment we stepped into the visitation area a chill ran down my spine. The harsh fluorescent lights cast a sterile, unwelcoming glare over everything. Behind the thick plexiglass, I saw Jordan, his face bruised and swollen, a stark testament to the confrontational nature of his arrest. His eyes, once full of life, now seemed dulled by the uncertainty and fear that clung to him like a shadow.

I would be the first to say that awaiting sentencing in county jail is a unique form of torture. The unknown looms large; you have no idea how much time you will receive or where in the state you will be sent to serve your sentence. The air felt heavy with a mix of anxiety and resignation, the walls seeming to close in around you.

Every visit felt like a step into another world—a world where time stands still and hope is fragile and fleeting.

R-Units

The Receiving Units are intense and highly regimented environments where every inmate in the state of Washington goes through an assessment process before being assigned to a permanent facility. This stage determines the security level and appropriate prison for each individual based on various factors such as their criminal history, behavior, and personal needs. Jordan once shared with me the reality of this process: You might find yourself sharing a cell with someone who is only serving a short one-year sentence or with a person sentenced to life imprisonment. The unpredictability and diverse backgrounds of fellow inmates make the Receiving Units a challenging and tense experience for everyone involved.

My weekly visits often made *me* feel like the criminal. The experience was unnerving, starting with the pat-downs by the guards, strict reminders to keep our hands visible above the tables at all times, and the prohibition of any physical contact such as handshakes or hugs. However, these discomforts paled in comparison to the reality Jordan described: inmates spend 23 hours a day confined to their cells with just one hour allotted to yard time. In these cells, three men are crammed into a space measuring only six by eight feet, creating an environment of extreme confinement and minimal personal space. This glimpse into the harsh conditions underscores the profound loss of liberty experienced by those incarcerated.

As time passed, Jordan's patience wore thin. He anxiously awaited the decision on which prison would become his final destination for the remainder of his sentence. My mind was haunted by scenes from films like *Shawshank Redemption*, *The Hurricane*, and *The Count of Monte Cristo*, as I imagined the grim realities of Jordan's new home. Given the nature of his offense, I knew he would likely be spared from the harshest environments of maximum-security prisons like Walla Walla or other high-security facilities in Washington. Despite the uncertainty, I held onto the belief that God works in mysterious ways. Finally, the State of Washington determined that Jordan would spend the next year and a half at McNeil Island Corrections Center. This medium-security prison, located on an island, provided some solace in knowing that while his situation was far from ideal, it was not the worst possible outcome.

Jordan,   MAY 7, 2010

I hope this brief note finds you well. I have heard bits and pieces of your transition to Shelton through Mom. I also heard the good news regarding Jeremiah and (did I get this right?) him receiving a sentence of 20 months. I am sure you must be very relieved and thankful for your friend.

The Hillis' gathered yesterday at our crib to celebrate Mother's Day. One of the things that came up (from Aunt Kathy) was the idea of everyone in the family creating a CD of their favorite 10 songs. We had some good time talking about whose CD would have what on it, ranging from Uncle Mark's commitment to rock (Zeppelin), Aunt Cheryl's love of Christian to Kasi's love of country. In the end we all decided that your boy Tupac would probably come up more than any other artist. One of the goals is that we will create an overall CD and, if this is possible, send it to you.

I hoped you enjoyed the Mary Oliver poem I sent you. I am sending another one (you can probably tell she is one of my favorites). This one is called "When Death Comes" and I am sending it to you because you remind me of some of its deep truths. The first is Mary's unflinching understanding that death comes to us all when she writes, "When death comes like the hungry bear in autumn." It is, as many have said, the great equalizer. I have always appreciated the way you, similar to Mary, have been willing to look death straight in the eye.

The second thing she surfaces is the posture by which she wants to be found when death does come. As she states so beautifully,

"I want to step through the door full of curiosity, wondering: what is it going to be like, that cottage of darkness?" It seems to me she is stating that we can face this reality of death in different ways and she wants to take the path that is life-giving. I have been deeply challenged by this attitude in you of taking the positive road.

Finally she makes a number of statements of what looking at death with curiosity will mean through an array of behavior. The one that struck me most in light of you was where she writes, "I don't want to end up simply having visited this world." I don't know about you Jo, but I think of how true this statement is for so many where they didn't live in the world, they just visited it by never risking, challenging themselves, willing to get scraped up, etc. Whatever else anybody could or would say to you, no one can question whether you have lived! You have deeply challenged me to live rather than just visit. Thank you for that great gift.

Your boy who loves you deeply, D

When Death Comes
By Mary Oliver

When death comes
like the hungry bear in autumn;
when death comes and takes all the bright coins from his purse

to buy me, and snaps the purse shut;
when death comes
like the measles-pox

when death comes
like an iceberg between the shoulder blades,

I want to step through the door full of curiosity, wondering:
what is it going to be like, that cottage of darkness?

And therefore I look upon everything
as a brotherhood and a sisterhood,
and I look upon time as no more than an idea,
and I consider eternity as another possibility,

and I think of each life as a flower, as common
as a field daisy, and as singular,

and each name a comfortable music in the mouth
tending as all music does, toward silence,

and each body a lion of courage, and something
precious to the earth.

When it's over, I want to say all my life
I was a bride married to amazement.
I was the bridegroom, taking the world into my arms.

When it is over, I don't want to wonder
if I have made of my life something particular, and real.

I don't want to find myself sighing and frightened,
or full of argument.

I don't want to end up simply having visited this world.

Jordan, MAY 14, 2010

Greetings my young brother and I hope this short letter finds you well. As always, I want you to know my prayers are with you and I hope and trust they are serving you with some kind of comfort and encouragement.

Thank you for the wonderful letter. I appreciated you taking the time to describe your workout; your willingness to forgo trashy "Nana novels" and, consequently, your choice of National Geographic (which would make your Uncle Mark very happy); your reading of Mary's poem every night; and your remembrance of our time in Thailand.

It was a remarkable time, was it not? There are so many memories of that trip that I cherish, but the one that you may not even remember was in Chiang Rai after we had returned from a night with Akhas. If you remember, you and I needed a serious beer and we went down to the bar. As we were kicking back and enjoying a cold one, I looked over at you and saw you staring off toward the street. What struck me was how relaxed your face looked. You had, if you remember, been pretty tense the couple of months prior to the trip. In seeing your face so relaxed I was overwhelmed with my perception of your peacefulness and the good plans God ultimately has for you. I have continued to go back to that picture of you many times to remind me of what I deeply believe to be a very hopeful future for you.

I am glad you like Mary. You are correct: She is a very deep soul. One of the things I like so much about her is how she takes very simple things that we take for granted and, as you and rappers like to say, "flips them" to reveal a deeper truth. It is that same quality I have always perceived is at play in your poetry where you take something common (like streetlights) and reveal how they have deeper meaning (their ability to be indiscriminate on everyone).

I am sending you another of her poems called "The Fist" which is a favorite of mine. I particularly like the way she writes about how many of us see our environment as a 'fist of God's' when in fact (if we get our eyes checked) what is really happening are open hands that become 'an invitation.' I don't know if you know, but for many years I have had a bronze sculpture of a pair of open hands that hold a globe of the earth. It is my way of remembering that no matter how bad it gets, somewhere, deep down and often difficult to see, there is a goodness that holds us up. I pray that you see that in both your current reality as well as the rest of your life.

Your boy who has your back, D

The Fist
By Mary Oliver

There are days
when the sun goes down
like a fist,
though of course

if you see anything
in the heavens this way
you had better get

your eyes checked
or, better still,
your diminished spirit.
The heavens

have no fist,
or wouldn't they have been
shaking it
for a thousand years now,

and even
longer than that,
at the dull, brutish
ways of mankind—

heaven's own
creation?
Instead: such patience!
Such willingness

to let us continue!
To hear,
little by little,
the voices—

only, so far, in
pockets of the world—
suggesting the possibilities

of peace?
Keep looking.
Behold, how the fist opens
with invitation.

Jordan, MAY 21, 2010

What up boy? I received some reports from Ryan and Mom that you are looking a bit scruffy these days? In fact Ryan told me that he had never seen anybody with so many cowlicks in their hair! I laughed myself to sleep just thinking about your ass.

I hope this last week has gone well for you. I heard that you were a bit discouraged about some of the results from the tests they gave you. Keep your head up. Truth be told if any of us took those tests we would probably have a harder time with them than you can imagine. The other thing is intelligence comes in many guises of which tests are one very small part. You are—and this is no bullshit—one of the most thoughtful, insightful, and reflective people I have ever met. I have no doubt that you will find your intellectual home in the future.

I am sending you another poem that I think you might like. It is by Dietrich Bonhoeffer who was a German pastor during the time of Hitler. Because of what he saw taking place with the Jews he decided to assassinate Hitler by placing a bomb in his office. The plot failed (the bomb was kicked behind the leg of a table which protected Hitler), but Bonhoeffer was arrested and ultimately put to death. This poem I am sending you is one he wrote while he was in prison awaiting his death. The reason I like it is because he captures for me how I often feel, where what I am like to others on the outside is very different from the way I feel on the inside. I also like the fact that he never answers the question the way I think he would (by deciding between the two alternatives), but actually goes for a third option which is that he is God's. I hope this is of some help while you, similar to Bonhoeffer, find yourself in the cell.

Finally, I hope you know how deeply missed you are. No day goes by without me thinking about you and wishing you were around. I am also very mindful that when you do come back to us you will be a bigger, deeper, and wiser person because of your experience.

Your boy, D

Who Am I?[11]
By Dietrich Bonhoeffer

Who am I? They often tell me
I stepped from my cell's confinement
calmly, cheerfully, firmly,
like a squire from his country house.

Who am I? They often tell me
I used to speak to my warders
freely and friendly and clearly,
as though it were mine to command.

Who am I? They also tell me
I bore the days of misfortune
equally, smilingly, proudly,
like one accustomed to win.

Am I then really all that which other men tell of?
Or am I only what I myself know of myself?
Restless and longing and sick, like a bird in a cage,
struggling for breath, as though hands were compressing
    my throat,
yearning for colors, for flowers, for the voices of birds,
thirsting for words of kindness, for neighborliness,

11 Dietrich Bonhoeffer, *Letters and Papers from Prison*, ed. Eberhard Bethge (NY Touchstone, 1997), 347.

trembling with anger at despotism and petty humiliation,
tossing in expectation of great events,
powerlessly trembling for friends at an infinite distance,
weary and empty at praying, at thinking, at making,
faint, and ready to say farewell to it all?

Who am I? This or the other?
Am I one person today, and tomorrow another?
Am I both at once? A hypocrite before others,
and before myself a contemptibly woebegone weakling?
Or is something within me still like a beaten army,
fleeing in disorder from a victory already achieved?

Who am I? They mock me, these lonely questions of mine.
Whoever I am, thou knowest, O God, I am thine!

MISHPACHA REFLECTIONS
The Dap
By Colin McArthur, Friend

When I think of Jordan Hillis I think of the moment (re-lived countless times) when we'd first see each other and he'd dap me up.[12] I loved this moment with JO because, unlike anybody I ever met, he started the dap process yards away from me each time. We would have to take several steps before interlocking thumbs[13], which meant we were in a half-motion promenade toward each other for sometimes as far as 10 feet. I can still see Jordan as clear as day, his right hand raised shoulder high, fingers splayed as far apart as they could go, like he was trying to grab as much of something as he could. I want to think he was showing me how much he cared for me in that simple moment, like a child that stretches their arms apart to show you the muchness of their love. How much did Jordan love me? As far apart as a human can stretch their hand waiting for a dap. He'd swing that hand toward mine and pull me in, clap me on the back and say (I can still hear it), "What's up, big bro?"

I hear his voice—that Tacoma-born, Tacoma-bred growl. When he was first released from jail, I helped orchestrate a job for him at my mother-in-law's meat packing plant. Her first question to me was, "Why does he talk like that?"[14] I acted like it wasn't a big deal, but in reality, Jordan's cadence and the

---

12 "Dap up" is slang for a handshake that consists of clasping hands in arm-wrestling fashion, palm to palm and pulling each other in for a half "bro hug." These are ambiguous terms for concrete acts that I assure you every human under the age of 45 in the city of Tacoma knows.
13 Critical component of the dap
14 My mother-in-law is a fantastic woman who, along with her husband, employed Jordan while he got on his feet after his release. She, like me, just did not grow up on the Hilltop in Tacoma and finds the dialect somewhat odd.

things he said charmed me from the beginning. In a toast to his soon-to-be-married brother, in front of his grandfather, Jordan repeated in that growl, "Yo ass done good. Yo ass done so good." How could I resist?

The open, welcoming palm and the gravel and bourbon voice calling me "big bro" paled in comparison to what happened on Jordan's face each time we greeted each other—a smile spread across his entire face and his broad forehead[15] erupted with happy wrinkles. The "happy" is an important distinction, because if you hadn't seen the opposite of this joyful-Jordan look, you might not be able to appreciate how beautiful this happy version of Jordan was[16]. Those moments are the simple times I cherish. The moments where Jordan was eager to love, eager to be joyful, and eager for family and community. Jordan was that so very much of the time... except when he wasn't.

Two of the final times I saw Jordan illuminated this dichotomy in ways that are burned into my memory as clear as that look on his face, as clear as the fingers on his outstretched hand. The first instance doesn't need much air time other than to say Jordan was not eager to love, he was not eager to be joyful. It was a dark moment that sucked the air out of an entire day. At the moment it felt surreal[17] in a way that I wasn't quite sure

---

15 That forehead, a gene-based gift from Sweet D

16 I once saw JO call his friend at roughly 3 a.m. and berate the friend's voicemail that he needed to "get his ass up" and "call me right fucking now" to clear the air regarding the failed high school romance of one of Jordan's brothers and this friend, who was then dating the high school ex. Not happy forehead lines.

17 To know Jordan was to know that he was somewhat unpredictable. I never experienced this directly, as I often flew under the radar when things were volatile, but I saw it plenty of times. I watched him slap the bejesus out of one of his brothers on that brother's birthday in a shadow boxing game gone wrong. It wasn't mean, just off. And when things got off for Jo, sometimes they got way off.

how to recover from. We parted ways, him to his anger and stubbornness, me to my confusion and fear.

The next time I saw Jordan it was a little over a week later when we were asked to demo a house for another friend.[18] Dozens of us showed up to work on this house and I saw Jordan pull up. He was wearing a gray tank top and walked straight toward me. The last time I had seen him he was manic, couldn't be talked to and, quite frankly, scary. When he was about 10 feet from me his right hand shot up, hand as big as a dinner plate and his face broke into the beam of light that eased all concern and made you want to hold him close as long as he'd let you for the sheer joy of it.

"What's up, big bro," he said, and before I could pull away he continued, "I'm sorry for last week." It was a simple statement in a simple embrace. A simple act that will stay with me forever.

I stammered something about how it wasn't a big deal and water under the bridge and I'd already forgotten[19]. But in that moment what I was feeling was immense gratitude. Gratitude that I was family enough to Jordan to be let into this simple kindness of a genuine embrace, an apology when none was necessary, and a moment to erase the darkness. In that time, and in every moment I think about Jordan, it's so simple and good. God bless the man who knows he's living in simple times.

---

18 You'll see a theme here: Jordan had a million friends and he was in communication with them all, whether it be to help in a last minute demo of a house, or to threaten their livelihood in the middle of the night.

19 Obviously this isn't true because I'm recounting it to you as if it were yesterday.

Jo,   MAY 28, 2010

Greetings my brother and I hope this past week has been good
for you. It sounds as though you and Ryan had a very good
time together. I have sent in my stuff and am waiting to hear if
they have approved me. With my past one never knows.

Have you been putting pencil to paper as to any poems? How
is the reading of National Geographic going? I have a number
of books I am prepared to send you when you are allowed to
receive them. In particular, I am going to send you a book by
a guy whose name is Sherman Alexie. He is a Native American
who grew up on the Spokane Reservation and now lives in
Seattle and is married to an old colleague of mine. He is a deep
truth teller and funny as hell. He has written a number of books,
but the one I am going to send to you first is called *The Toughest
Indian In the World*. I think you will enjoy it a great deal.

I am doing pretty well. My job has its ups and downs. One of
the things that makes it tough is raising the money we need.
We have a woman who is thinking about giving Leadership
Foundations a large gift. I would appreciate your prayers for
this. It has been good to have Ryan living with us. He is doing
a good job at work, he has been running with Uncle Mike and
Aunt Kathy, and playing a bit of basketball on a team. While
Patrick is in South Africa we have a standing call each Tuesday
morning where we chop it up for a bit and talk about you, him
and Teresa, the upcoming World Cup, and his soul.

I am, once again, sending you another poem. It is by another
of my favorites, Denise Levertov. This poem, "City Psalm,"

reminds me a lot of the one you wrote about streetlights. I particularly like where she writes, "I have seen not behind but within, within the dull grief, blown grit, hideous concrete facades, another grief, a gleam as of dew, an abode of mercy." I have always thought this is one of your great strengths, not turning your head away from the tough things and, even more, to see light in the dark.

I would be interested to know what you think about this poem and, specifically, what you think about the phrase "an abode of mercy"? Would you say you have experienced mercy in your life? If so, how? And if not, why not?

In a couple of weeks I will be headed to the monastery to hang out with "my monks." I look forward to taking you up there when you get out. I think you will find the place very conducive to the things that matter to you.

Your boy, D

City Psalm
By Denise Levertov

The killings continue, each second
pain and misfortune extend themselves
in the genetic chain, injustice is done knowingly, and the air
bears the dust of decayed hopes,
yet breathing those fumes, walking the thronged
pavements among crippled lives, jackhammers
raging, a parking lot painfully agleam
in the May sun, I have seen
not behind but within, within the
dull grief, blown grit, hideous
concrete facades, another grief, a gleam
as of dew, an abode of mercy,
have heard not behind but within noise
a humming that drifted into a quiet smile.
Nothing was changed, all was revealed otherwise;
not that horror was not, not that the killings did not continue,
not that I thought there was to be no more despair,
but that as if transparent all disclosed
an otherness that was blessed, that was bliss.
I saw Paradise in the dust of the street.

SUMMER

Jo,   JUNE 4, 2010

I hope you are well, my young brother. It was wonderful to talk with you this past weekend and hear your perspective on life, get caught up on your workout regime, listen to you talk about this older guy you walk the yard with—all good stuff.

I was particularly encouraged by your sense of "keeping some of the things you are thinking to yourself." I think this is a very sensible move on your part. As you and I have both talked about in the past, there is way too much talk in this world and not enough action. One of the phrases I love in the Bible is where Mary (who becomes the mother of Jesus) is first told by an angel that she is going to birth the savior of this world. It says that she "pondered these things in her heart"[20], which I take to mean she went underground and thought hard, long, and deep. It seems to me that you, too, are "pondering some things in your heart" these days. This is a wise move. Speaking of all that, I am going up to the monastery next week to hang out with "my monks." I look forward to when you get out and we can go get some time together at the monastery.

The poem of this week is from none other than your boy, P-Did. That fool sent me this poem after he finished *Let the Great World Spin*. Because of Corrigan reminding him of you (and me also), he spit this out. I think P has some of your skills. I love the way he starts it with your comment at the bedside of JD at the hospital. Do you remember saying, "Let me take his place"? I sure do. It was one of the most holy moments of

---

20 Luke 2:19

my life. His other line of "small beauties dressed in garments of tragedy" is also a very strong piece of writing where he clearly is referring to JD's death, but I also think many other things like Mom's health issues, some of the stuff you and your brothers have faced, my relationship with my dad, etc. His next line of "bruised and beaten up by life's midnight" is a wonderful turn of phrase where I instantly feel that this is exactly what has happened with me. And then of course his final phrase "fixes his eyes on the darkness… sees something he could only see… a glimmer of light" feels to me that it creates a sense of movement where we descend into darkness, recognize darkness, and then darkness becomes our help. Does this make sense? I think that he has captured you in a very strong and poetic way. Do you think so? If so, how? And if not, how not?

Pray for me this week while I am at the monastery. I need to get some rest and know (in my heart) that God is in control of this thing. I will pray for you, as always.

Lovingly, D

Poem for Jo[21]
By Patrick Hillis

Let me take his place!, he shouts,

sobbing bedside soaking sheets with tears

that could only be produced by life-lost-life-times-too-soon

Small beauties dressed in the garments of tragedy.

A moment in time,

suspended seven floors above the gravel and gutters of
    grimy streets,

the very place he would run to in search of a fully
    believable God.

From that day forward,

if light was to be discovered it could only be found in the
    darkest of places,

if it could be found at all.

And now, years later, bruised and beaten up by life's midnight,

he fixes his eyes on the darkness of this world and the
    darkness in his self,

and sees something he could only see from there—
    a glimmer of light.

---

21 Used with permission

Jo,   JUNE 11, 2010

Greetings my brother. I just got home and heard the good news—you got your time cut in half—wow! You must be becoming a regular believer in the power of prayer. You better watch out or the next thing we know you will be laying your hands on people and becoming a regular faith-healer.

My time at the monastery was good. I am looking forward to the day that I can take you with me. It is your kind of place, where you have a bunch of monks that have made some deep commitments to live life with integrity, transparency, and commitment. Whether one likes "what" they stand for, no one can deny "how" they stand up for it and represent.

While I was up there I, along with praying for you, continued to read the Jack Dempsey book. One of the reasons I do it is to stay connected to you in spirit, where I am reading something that you would read. A couple of things stood out in the book that I thought (and maybe you already know) you would find interesting. For example, did you know that back in the day there was no round limit? In other words, they stopped a fight not because of a certain number of rounds but when one boxer could not answer the bell. In the case of Jess Willard, he beat Jack Johnson in a fight in Cuba in the 26th round. Can you imagine? Earlier (the 1890's) a guy by the name of John "the Boston Strong Boy" Sullivan knocked out a guy in the 75th round. 75 freaking rounds! I cannot begin to imagine what kind of shape they must have been in. This brings me back to your boy Dempsey. As much as I respect him, I also have mad respect for Willard. In their initial fight, Dempsey hit him so hard that his jaw and cheek were broken into 13 different places. What is so impressive is that with his face smashed up, Willard continues to fight for another four rounds. Can you imagine continuing to fight like that? This is a great book and I am very thankful to you for recommending it to me.

What did you think about P-Did's poem? Pretty good, wasn't it? I have continued to encourage him (like I have encouraged you) to keep writing.

This week I have enclosed a poem called "Traveling with Jack Shit." It is about Reid Carpenter (who I think you have met), the guy whose place I took in becoming president of Leadership Foundations. The reason I like it (and I think you will as well) is that Reid is a living example of what you have talked about where we don't need to look or act a certain way to walk with God. Reid is a cigar-smoking (used to be cigarettes), scotch-drinking, cussing piece of humanity. And interestingly enough, one of the holiest guys I know. This poem tries to use the idea of Reid's commitment to "shit" as also the thing that makes him holy.

I will chat with you next week and again, congratulations on the great news.

Your boy, D

Traveling with Jack Shit[22]
For Reid Carpenter
By H. Spees

I've got this friend. His name is Jack… Jack Shit.

I'm on the road with him from time to time. And he always says "shit."

I mean not just says, "shit," but he's raised the articulation of the word to a frickin' art form. ("Frickin"… now that's another story… but not really.) He has, over the course of our travels, invested the word "shit" with every conceivable human emotion. The word can wing off the tip of his tongue like an ode to joy, or powerfully punctuate his passion. It can peek around the edges of a delightfully crude joke, or just sit in the middle of the floor when describing a hard reality.

For Jack, it's a style. A macho thing. But more.

It's a screen: Jack uses it as if to say, "If you can't handle my earthy vocabulary, don't waste my time, because there's deeper stuff than language you'll have to wade into and deal with if you travel with me."

It's a statement: People on the streets say "shit" a lot. And Jack knows a lot of people on the streets. "Shit," for Jack, says, "I accept all people. If you want me for a friend, it's best for you to know that up front."

---

22 Used with permission

I've watched my friend Jack carefully over time, and I've discovered something: The only word he enjoys saying more than "shit" is "Jesus."

And I believe it's significant. I don't know what it is, but I know there's a link somewhere deep in the recesses of Jack Shit's twisted mind. I know that there is some kind of—not logical—but organic connection, a meeting between shit and Jesus.

When Jack says "shit," it's like turning over tables and clearing out the temple. Just like nothing clears a room like a good, up-from-the-bottom-of-the-barrel fart, so nothing clears out tidy, judgmental, bail-out-when-the-going-gets-tough religious folks like "Shit!" yelled full-out, echoing off the walls.

For Jack, "shit" has spiritual power.

Like that day when they brought that lady (not the man) who they caught in the very act of adultery to Jesus. That shit Jesus was writing on the ground—the names, places, and dates scrawled in the dust—reminding those guys with rocks in their hands of the worst shit they'd done. The power of shit made those in the front rows drop their rocks and edge shamefacedly away from that lady and her shit-scribbling defender.

Or like all that shit floating in that cup Jesus was handed in the garden, the cup he asked the father to pass from him. The cup full of my shit. Your shit. Jack's shit.

I think Jack works off of a theology of shit that goes something like this:

There's only one person I can go to, in the end, who
when I am so full of shit my eyes are brown;
when I'm in deep shit, shit up to my neck, over my head;
when shit is running out my mouth because I have shit for
brains;
when I've just shit all over myself like a drunk lying in his own
puke because his wife, his last friend, just went to an AL-anon
meeting and refuses to clean him up for the 364th time this year;
when I'm up shit creek without a paddle;
when I'm shit out of luck;
when shit happens…
He's there,
waiting for me,
knowing how often I choose him last.

I don't know what to do with my friend Jack. He has other
habits too, like pulling his upper plate out of his mouth and
smiling a toothless smile at the most solemn times.

But I do know this: Jack's a good shit. In fact, Jack is Holy
Shit. Yes Holy. What Jack's life seems to be saying is something
profound, something like: "Jesus touched me, embraced
me, held me past the point of comfortability. He held me
till I squirmed; then held me till I broke down, limp in his
strong arms, his person pressing against mine, his acceptance
penetrating my body, my skin, my mind, my heart, my bones,
even the deepest bowels of my soul, those places dark with
stench, still full of self and sin and broken pieces, and all the
masticated garbage I've taken in over my life. He loves me and

my shit. He loves me in my shit. His acceptance invades it all and makes it all, all of me, Holy. Holy Shit."

That's why I like traveling with Jack. Because I know without a shadow of a doubt that if Jesus accepts a shithead like my friend Jack, there may be hope for me. And I know that if Jesus accepts Jack and Jack accepts me, then when I fear losing the hope inside, I can feel that hope, Jack's hope, beside me, until my own hope shines cleanly through my shit again.

Jo,

I hope this short note finds you well. I am still trying to heal from my beloved Celtics getting busted up last night by the hated Lakers. What makes the pain even more grievous is that I had to watch them get beat sitting next to your cousins, Cory and Matthew. And finally the most difficult part is that I owe Cory a dinner and, for the rest of the summer, every time I see Matthew I have to say, "You are my god." It's going to be rough!

And speaking of sports… as I write your boy P is at the US/ Slovenia World Cup match. I wonder how crazy that boy decided to get and whether he painted himself up, is blowing one of those horns, or got a bit lit before the game. He is capable of any and all of those behaviors as you well know!

Lastly (in the spirit of sports) your boy Chase had a scrimmage the other night and, while I did not make the game, Tad told me he was a beast on both sides of the ball. He caught two 50-yard touchdown passes and manned up at the corner position. Tad is very hopeful that Chase is going to have a very good year.

I am doing pretty well. Work is both full and a bit tiring. The good news is I have a good team to work with and I get to wake up each day doing work that matters for people in cities around the world that are often without much hope. The tough part is trying to get people to donate to support this work. Any prayers from you about this would be deeply appreciated.

My poem to you this week is actually more like a prayer. Although I should add that I believe good poetry is prayer and vice versa. All that to say this prayer/poem is from a monk by the name of Thomas Merton who I think you would like very much. I read a bit from him every morning and one of the things I like most about him is how brave he is. He is not afraid to tell God whatever is on his mind and heart—a lot like you. In particular, I love the transparency of saying, "he has no idea where he is going" and that he really doesn't "know himself." But the key line in my mind is his belief that "the desire to please you does in fact please you." It seems to me that in the end that is all we can really hope for: the right desire. This I should add is what I deeply believe about you. I am convinced that in your heart you have always had the desire—regardless of what has happened—to please. And that this pleases God about you. I see this manifested in your loyalty to friends and family; your love of literature; and your courage and righteous anger. All very pleasing to me, others, and God!

Your boy, D

A Prayer[23]
By Thomas Merton
From *Thoughts in Solitude*

MY LORD GOD,

I have no idea where I am going.

I do not see the road ahead of me.

I cannot know for certain where it will end.

Nor do I really know myself, and the fact that I think that

I am following your will does not mean that I am actually
doing so.

But I believe that the desire to please you does in fact please you.

And I hope I have that desire in all that I am doing.

I hope that I will never do anything apart from that desire.

And I know that if I do this you will lead me by the right road,
though I may know nothing about it.

Therefore will I trust you always, though I may seem to be lost
and in the shadow of death.

I will not fear, for you are ever with me, and you will never
leave me to face my perils alone.

---

23 Thomas Merton, *Thoughts in Solitude*, (NY: Farrar, Straus and Giroux, 199), 79.

Jordan,   JUNE 25, 2010

I hope you are well my young warrior! It has been quite a week
ranging from the wonderful call I received from you on Father's
Day to getting the crew off to South Africa (they left yesterday)
to celebrating Mom's birthday. Lots of good stuff, but I am
ready to rest this weekend.

Did you get a chance to watch the US/Algeria soccer game on
Wednesday? I did not know soccer could be so exciting. What
became even more interesting to me was discovering that the
goal keeper for the US team suffers from Tourette syndrome.
Did you know this? It appears by way of the interview that
his manifestation is similar to yours—the tics, stretching, etc.
What I also liked about the interview is how both of you as a
result of the syndrome have become "warriors" regarding your
focus and commitment. Good stuff!

I have been thinking a lot about our conversation on the
process of forgiveness. I think the fact that you have been able
to discover how important that is for you and others is a very
important first step. Of course the next step is how to put it
into action. I hope you had a chance to take me up on my
suggestion about writing people's names on a piece of paper,
the thing that they have done that you need to forgive them for,
and then tearing up the paper and flushing it down the toilet as
a way of saying you forgive them. I have done this many times,
both literally and symbolically.

The reason that this is so critical is that to the degree that we do
not forgive someone is to the degree that we give them power

over our life. Isn't that something? I know my natural reaction is when someone has hurt or dishonored me I often think the best way to get back at them is not to forgive them. But in fact what actually happens is that I give them control over me, which is the very thing they wanted in the first place. This is why I have made it a practice to forgive over and over again. I would like to know what you think about all of this.

To that end I am sending you a line from C.S. Lewis that captures this complicated relationship between forgiving others and being forgiven. He writes, "forgiving and being forgiven are two names for the same thing."[24] Easy to say, hard to do. Let's stay at it, broheim.

Your boy who's got your back, D

---

24 Eberhard Arnold, Dietrich Bonhoeffer, Mother Teresa, Martin L. King, C. S. Lewis, Wendell Berry, Richard Rohr, et al. *Following the Call: Living the Sermon on the Mount Together*. ed. Charles E. Moore (NY: Plough Publishing House, 2021), 230.

Jo,   JULY 2, 2010

I hope you are well and I just got the good news from Mom—
you are headed to McNeil. Another answer to prayer for you!
I think you and I should get our hustle on and begin to charge
money for prayers that we are seeing answered. What do you
think?

Thank you for the very nice birthday note. I deeply appreciate
you indicating to me that I have been a good role model. It is
something I have always wanted to be for you, your brothers,
and others, but have often felt that I am the farthest thing from
it. I hope if I have been able to show you anything it would
be what it means to live a life on behalf of others, see grace in
everything, and live out forgiveness. Beyond that there is not
much I know.

I am about a third of the way through your book, *Unforgivable
Blackness*. It is a remarkably good and sad story. It is good in
that Jack Johnson lived life in a way that all of us would hope
to—proud, genuine, and resolute—but very few of us do. It is
also very sad when one reflects on the depth of the racism that
our country has demonstrated (and still does). Particularly the
way the white fighters kept him out of the game when he was
clearly the best fighter in the world. It is also very well written.
Thanks for giving me the hook-up on this book and story.

I am looking forward to this weekend. As you know, the Fourth
of July is always a good time at the condo. I am also looking
forward to turning 52. I don't know what it is about this age,
but something tells me that this next year is going to be very

significant for the Hillis family and that my birthday will be the start of it.

My poem this week for you is from my favorite, Mary Oliver. It is called "Maybe." I like it for a variety of reasons, but particularly the way she describes Jesus. It begins with the line, "his melancholy madness" and then talks about the way he calms the physical storm. But more importantly, she ends it not with the storm, but with the "tender and luminous and demanding" nature of Jesus that is—and isn't this the truth—"a thousand times more frightening than the killer sea." I don't know about you, but this speaks very loudly to me. The things that I tend to think are really big around me—you guys, mom, my job—are not nearly as big as who this God is and what this God wants with my life. I hope you enjoy it.

Finally, I heard my last letter got returned for lack of a return address—my bad, Jo. I have stuck it in this envelope.

Have a great weekend and I will be thinking and praying for you. Please pray for me.

Your boy, D

Maybe
By Mary Oliver

Sweet Jesus, talking
　　his melancholy madness,
　　　　stood up in the boat
　　　　　　and the sea lay down,

silky and sorry.
　　So everybody was saved
　　　　that night.
　　　　　　But you know how it is

when something
　　different crosses
　　　　the threshold—the uncles
　　　　　　mutter together,

the women walk away,
　　the young brother begins
　　　　to sharpen his knife.
　　　　　　Nobody knows what the soul is.

It comes and goes
　　like the wind over the water—
　　　　sometimes, for days,
　　　　　　you don't think of it.

Maybe, after the sermon,
   after the multitude was fed,
      one or two of them felt
        the soul slip forth

like a tremor of pure sunlight
   before exhaustion,
      that wants to swallow everything,
        gripped their bones and left them

miserable and sleepy,
   as they are now, forgetting
      how the wind tore at the sails
        before he rose and talked to it—

tender and luminous and demanding
   as he always was—
      a thousand times more frightening
        than the killer sea.

Jordan,   JULY 9, 2010

By the time you receive this letter you will be in your new
surroundings at McNeil. I am already praying that your new
environment will be all that you hope it will be where, along
with the books we will now be able to send you (and please let
us know as soon as that is possible), you will get much more
time to exercise, be outside away from your cell, and be able
to see the good views that this place affords you. I also want to
let you know that your Uncle Mark and I jumped on the news
and have sent our forms in. We will let you know as soon as we
hear whether we are approved.

I will be very interested to hear from you about your feelings
regarding being in three different places, how you experienced
each one and what you learned, how they transport you, etc.

Well our good weather has finally come (and perfect timing for
you at McNeil). Are you handling the heat? What allowances
(if any) do they make for you all when it gets this hot? We will
be spending some time out at the lake this weekend.

By way of a poem this week I was thinking about one that could
properly baptize your new surroundings. The one I am sending
you, "The Guest House," is by one of my favorite poets—a
guy by the name of Rumi. Rumi was a 13th century Sufi (the
mystical form of Islam) who had a deep love for the truth—
whether Islamic, Christian, etc. In this poem he creates a great
metaphor where he turns humans into a guest house and then,
similar to a guest house, describes how we should live. The
idea, of course, is that a guest house does not discriminate, but

welcomes anyone who decides to stay there. Similarly, one of the things that I am trying to do is take all the things that come to the "door" of my life and welcome them like they were honored guests. This has been particularly helpful for me as it relates to Mom's health issues, when you guys have gotten in trouble, and when I look at my own shit. If I can learn to be grateful for them like the poem describes, perhaps I can view them as guides that "are clearing me out for some new delight." I will pray this poem for you, Jo, and that you encounter your "new guest house." I pray that you "will welcome and entertain them all."

Your boy, D

The Guest House[25]
By Jalaluddin Rumi
Translation by Coleman Barks

This being human is a guest house.
Every morning a new arrival.

A joy, a depression, a meanness,
some momentary awareness comes
as an unexpected visitor.

Welcome and entertain them all!
Even if they're a crowd of sorrows,
who violently sweep your house
empty of its furniture,
still, treat each guest honorably.
He may be clearing you out
for some new delight.

The dark thought, the shame, the malice,
meet them at the door laughing,
and invite them in.

Be grateful for whoever comes,
because each has been sent
as a guide from beyond.

25 Coleman Barks, *The Essential Rumi - Reissue: New Expanded Edition* (San Francisco: Harper Collins, 1995) 109. Copyright © 1995 Coleman Barks. Used with permission.

MISHPACHA REFLECTIONS
The Island
By Ryan Hillis, Brother

From county jail to the R-Units, Jordan finally arrived at McNeil Island Corrections Center, a remote fortress in the Puget Sound. Visitors like myself would take a short ferry ride, a journey that became a lifeline for both Jordan and I, allowing us to spend precious hours together. I became a weekly visitor, eagerly anticipating my time on "the island," as we affectionately called it.

The history of McNeil Island is enough to send shivers down your spine; it once housed infamous inmates like Charles Manson and Mickey Cohen. Yet, before its closure, McNeil Island transitioned to housing inmates with less than five years remaining on their sentences. Compared to Jordan's first few months in jail, "the island" was like the long-awaited summer months in Tacoma. At McNeil, there was a glimmer of hope—a sense that the end of the tunnel was in sight. The prison was enveloped in a rugged, natural beauty, with the surrounding waters of the Puget Sound shimmering under the sun.

On "the island," Jordan and his fellow inmates experienced a semblance of freedom. They were assigned jobs, engaged in recreational activities, and enjoyed less restrictive visitations. Jordan used his time to deepen his faith, and he became something of a legend in both the gym and on the track. I remember sending him a pair of Reebok running shoes the first chance I got. Jordan always stomped around the streets of Tacoma in a size 13, but the closest size I could find in the commissary was 15.

The moment the shoes arrived, Jordan began training as a marathon runner. After his release, he would go on to run over five marathons, including the Boston Marathon twice. He quickly earned the nickname "Jericho Miles." I vividly recall the story he told of running the track during a snowy afternoon, the snowflakes thick and heavy, inches of snow accumulating on his head and shoulders. With each lap, his oversized shoes crunched through the snow, leaving deep imprints in the white blanket. His breath steamed in the cold air, a testament to his determination and endurance. Jordan's commitment to running became a symbol of his resilience, a beacon of hope and strength amid the confines of prison life.

Jordan,   JULY 16, 2010

I trust this letter finds you well. I heard through Mom that you arrived at McNeil, ran into my friend Shod, and are already looking at jobs ranging from the fire department to working on the boats. It sounds like you have been able to move in as well as could possibly be expected.

Things are good here. The crew just returned from South Africa so we have had a chance to hear some great stories about your boy, P. Both Ryan and I asked them if he had developed an accent (you know how P rolls) and was trying to act like Africa was his motherland. They did indicate that he had led them on a couple of tours, showed them how to shake hands like a South African, and took them to a couple of his favorite drinking establishments. All classic P-Did! More importantly though and in all seriousness, it sounds as though he has done a pretty marvelous job with his responsibilities. If you remember, P came up with the idea of creating a film school to teach kids in the city who are poor how to write a script, curate film footage, and edit. A few people from the crew said it was so good that they are thinking of trying to create something like that here in T-Town. I will be very interested to talk with P about his experience when he and Teresa return home which, if you can believe it, is July 29th.

I continue to plow through *Unforgivable Blackness*. I just finished the chapter where Johnson wins the heavyweight championship of the world. I did not know that he literally had to chase the guy down and, upon catching up with him, had to fight him in Australia because America wouldn't allow for such a thing.

Unbelievable! In reading the story I find myself having a deep respect for what he went through, had to overcome, and persevere through. What I am not sure about is whether I actually like him as a person. For example, I liked Jack Dempsey a lot, but I am not too sure about Johnson. We will see by the end of the book.

The poem I am sending you this week is called "Contraband" by Denise Levertov (whose poem, "City Psalm" I sent you earlier). I will be interested to see if you like it, but one of the reasons I am sending it to you is because her description of where God lives ("on the other side of the mirror"), and where we can see him ("through the slit where the barrier doesn't quite touch the ground") as God is ("filtered light"), seems to me a possible description of what you are living through. I am sure it must be hard at times to see God in your context. Perhaps God will be seen by you in those "slits" that you are surrounded by. At least this is my heartfelt prayer.

I love you Jo and am looking forward to seeing you as soon as my papers are approved.

Pax, D

Contraband
By Denise Levertov

The tree of knowledge was the tree of reason.
That's why the taste of it
drove us from Eden. That fruit
was meant to be dried and milled to a fine powder
for use a pinch at a time, a condiment.
God had probably planned to tell us later
about this new pleasure.
We stuffed our mouths full of it,
gorged on *but* and *if* and *how* and again
but, knowing no better.
It's toxic in large quantities; fumes
swirled in our heads and around us
to form a dense cloud that hardened to steel,
a wall between us and God, Who was Paradise.
Not that God is unreasonable—but reason
in such excess was tyranny
and locked us into its own limits, a polished cell
reflecting our own faces. God lives
on the other side of that mirror,
but through the slit where the barrier doesn't
quite touch ground, manages still
to squeeze in—as filtered light,
splinters of fire, a strain of music heard
then lost, then heard again

Jordan,   JULY 23, 2010

Well, first things first…I am rolling around T-Town in your ride. You will be happy to know that it is in very good shape. I promise to take very good care of it so as to have you riding in style upon your return. The only thing I can't promise is whether you will appreciate the tunes I decide to play. Although I know you enjoy jazz which I will definitely be playing, I am not sure whether you have become an aficionado of classical—have you? More particularly, I have a specific love of music that features cellos and oboes. Both of these instruments seem to tap into something almost primordial for me. There is a sadness woven through with sweetness; a simplicity punctuated with elegance; a heroic that is undergirded by the common. All stuff that you—in one form or another—have tattooed on your body. I hope you will fall in love with these two instruments as well!

As to Hillis news, two things might interest you. Patrick and Teresa come home next Thursday. I am looking forward to seeing them and hearing what will undoubtedly be P's wild ass, partly made-up stories. In talking with some of the people who saw them over there, it sounds like it was a very good, but also very hard experience. On a related note, have you received any word whether Patrick and I have been approved to come and see you? I sent my stuff as soon as you got transferred and we sent Patrick's stuff in this week. The second thing that you will appreciate (and maybe Ryan has already told you) is your cousin Whitney's 21st birthday. She decided to throw a beer-pong tournament and, low and behold, Ryan and Kasi won the tournament and the $150 jackpot. Even more exciting was the way they won. They were down two cups and on their final turn Ryan hit his and then Kasi hit hers for the win. It was very enjoyable to watch. We (the uncles) also took Whit out for her "Scotch experience."

This week instead of sending you poetry I am going to send you the conclusion to my doctoral thesis. The reason I do so is you figure prominently in it because I retell the story of JD's death and the basketball court. I was both deeply moved and awestruck by the way in which God used you to create JD's court. If it had not been for you there would be no court, no annual tournament, and no memory. Thank you once again for your role in all of this. I hope you enjoy. I will chat with you next week.

Your boy,

D

MISHPACHA REFLECTIONS
T-Town
By Cornelius Williams, Friend

Jordan's memory evokes a deep love because it embodies Tacoma.

Tacoma. You either love it or you don't and that goes for all the people that grew up here. It is historically a blue-collar town and attracted people from all over the country to work in its pulp and paper mill, animal-rendering plant, oil refinery, or aluminum smelter. People worked hard together, partied hard together, fought each other, and yet they stood together against anyone that disrespected us. We were down for T-Town.

Tacoma is also home to the Fort Lewis Army Base, McChord Air Force Base, and Camp Murray Army Base with the Washington Army National Guard, Washington State Guard, and Washington Air National Guard. It consistently attracted people from all over the country who were trained to live together, work together, fight together, and be prepared to stand against anyone at a moment's notice. Many in the military would finish their term of service and make Tacoma their home.

One other thing you should know about people from Tacoma—we have a chip on our shoulder. Most of us felt like no one saw us or respected us. People would even make fun of how our city smelled. They would drive through and make sure their windows were rolled up because of the "aroma of Tacoma." It did not matter to us what other people thought. We loved deeply, we loved our own (Eastside, Hilltop, Southside, etc.), and we did not take anything from anyone because we were down for T-Town. Yes, Jordan is Tacoma.

Jordan was still young when I moved away from Tacoma. I recall fond memories when I would go over to the Hillis home and play full court basketball in their backyard. Jordan was the youngest of the boys, but he was scrappy. He would get out there with us and try his best to hang, which I loved. I cannot recall him ever backing down. Even as a young guy, I saw the spirit of the city in him. The challenge and opportunity that Jordan would have to face is how he would harness that spirit of our city.

Throughout the years, I maintained my relationship with Jordan's dad who would periodically give me an update on Jordan. Some of the updates were good, the other ones were not so good. Trying to harness what was in him was a tough journey that created many wounds along the way for himself and those around him.

Wounds. Deep wounds. Yeah, this is part of being from Tacoma that no one talks about, and it is palpable. Those wounds create the chip, the edge, the angst, that at a moment's notice can be unleashed and hurt everything in its way. What most people do not understand is that underneath all those wounds are people that love deeply and want to be loved. That is why people from Tacoma look out for their own (however they decide who this is). That is why we take up for those that are overlooked. Because most of us from Tacoma love it deeply. Jordan is Tacoma.

There is nothing more beautiful than to hear the stories of people from Tacoma that have learned to harness the spirit of our city, especially when it has been surrendered to the Holy Spirit. People have gone on to help other people within Tacoma and beyond face challenges on their journey to become better. Just recently, Jordan's dad was providing support to another family because of the lessons learned while on the journey with his son. Jordan's life continues to inspire to love deeply and fight for others so that the wound can be healed and lead to good. Because that is what people from Tacoma do.

Jordan,

I am looking forward to seeing you tomorrow. In fact, by the time you read this Ryan, your Uncle Mark, and I will have already swooped through McNeil to chat it up a bit.

I have been thinking about you quite a bit this past week. Of course this is a rather odd thing to say because I think about you every day. For some particular reason—and I think this has mostly to do with our conversation on the phone over the weekend—I have felt a heavier burden than usual. Specifically, you made mention on the phone in relation to writing (or not writing) Nana that "you don't feel like you have much to say." This statement struck me in a very strong way for a couple of reasons. The first is that you are such a remarkably deep thinker that I am always under the impression that people around you have heard a fraction of what you think and feel. The second is that the way you phrase things is very unique. With this in mind I ran to a particular poem I am sending you that helped me gain a sense of what might be going on with you. It is called "The Beautiful, Striped Sparrow" by Mary Oliver.

The first thing that struck me was her line "in church they could not tame me, they would not keep me." I have often thought that a significant theme in your life is institutions—whether the church, school, work, etc.—trying to tame you, but you would not let them. Sometimes for good and sometimes for bad, but they definitely don't tame you. The second is the poem's acknowledgement that, although the church could not tame her, they were correct that "God, once he is in your heart, is everywhere." This is such a significant theme of your life. As

I have mentioned in previous letters, you, more than anyone, have taught me the truth of God being in places that I could not formerly imagine. But the most important lines in the poem and the ones that made me think of you are, "Am I lonely? The beautiful, striped sparrow, serenely, on the tallest weed in his kingdom, also sings without words." The acknowledged fact of "loneliness" must be a very real reality for you. I can't imagine the levels you must be dealing with this reality. But similar to the "sparrow" that uses this loneliness to "sing," I have a deep sense that this is true for you as well and, most importantly, "without words." It is this idea of "without words" that made me reflect on our conversation over the weekend. As opposed to you feeling bad about not being able to write, maybe what is going on in you is a "singing" that goes beyond words.

This is my deep prayer for you Jo: that you will see yourself as this "beautiful, striped sparrow... who sings without words."

Your boy,

D

The Beautiful, Striped Sparrow
By Mary Oliver

in the afternoons,
in the almost empty fields,
I hum the hymns
I used to sing

in church.
they could not tame me,
so they would not keep me,
alas,

and how that feels,
the weight of it,
i will not tell
any of you,

not ever.
still, as they promised,
God, once he is in your heart,
is everywhere—

so even here
among the weeds
and the brisk trees.
how long does it take

to hum a hymn? strolling
one or two acres
of the sweetness
of the world,

not counting
a lapse, now and again,
of sheer emptiness.
once a deer

stood quietly at my side.
and sometimes the wind
has touched my cheek
like a spirit.

am i lonely?
the beautiful, striped sparrow,
serenely, on the tallest weed in his kingdom,
also sings without words.

Jo,   AUGUST 6, 2010

This letter is going to come to you a bit earlier than typical given that I will be on vacation this week so I won't be in my office to write you as I usually do on Fridays.

It was wonderful to see you on Saturday. Mark, Ryan, and I have all remarked about how much we enjoyed the time and our sense that we were encountering in both your presence and your words something very holy. In particular, your statements regarding "bitterness" and letting it go so you aren't a miserable old man someday to "not wasting any time on people who aren't going to like you anyway" to "behaving like an old man (exercise, reading, and chess) to survive inside" were all words that we are going to think about for some time to come. Thanks for the gift of your wisdom.

I also wanted to tell you how much I respect your commitment to staying on a regiment while you are inside. It seems to me (at least I would be tempted this way) that it would be very easy either to sleep your time away or spend untold hours in front of the television. The way you are approaching this challenges me to be a better steward of my time.

To that end the poem I am sending you this week is by Rudyard Kipling. I don't know if you remember him, but among other things, he was the one who wrote *The Jungle Book* series. Do you remember watching this as a movie when you were little? Anyway, he wrote a poem called "If—" that I thought about during our time with you on Saturday. He premises the whole poem on a few things that remind me of what you are so admirably demonstrating. The first is that to be noble is not living in either extreme but in the middle, where you can keep your head when they are losing theirs and blaming it on you. The second is that to be noble is to have a will "and so hold on when there is nothing in you except the will which says to them: "Hold on!" And finally that it all depends on forgiveness which "if you can fill the unforgiving minute with sixty seconds' worth of distance run" will make you a man. It is this last idea—forgiveness becoming the key to maturity—which I am very encouraged by in you. I deeply sense, Jo, that you are learning how to forgive yourself and others. Once this lesson is learned, the sky is the limit.

Your boy who loves you deeply,

D

If—
By Rudyard Kipling

If you can keep your head when all about you
    Are losing theirs and blaming it on you;
If you can trust yourself when all men doubt you,
    But make allowance for their doubting too;
If you can wait and not be tired by waiting,
    Or, being lied about, don't deal in lies,
Or, being hated, don't give way to hating,
    And yet don't look too good, nor talk too wise:

If you can dream—and not make dreams your master;
    If you can think—and not make thoughts your aim;
If you can meet with Triumph and Disaster
    And treat those two imposters just the same;
If you can bear to hear the truth you've spoken
    Twisted by knaves to make a trap for fools,
Or watch the things you gave your life to, broken,
    And stoop and build 'em up with worn-out tools;

If you can make one heap of all your winnings
    And risk it on one turn of pitch-and-toss,
And lose, and start again at your beginnings
    And never breathe a word about your loss;
If you can force your heart and nerve and sinew
    To serve your turn long after they are gone,

And so hold on when there is nothing in you
    Except the Will which says to them: "Hold on";

If you can talk with crowds and keep your virtue,
    Or walk with kings—nor lose the common touch;
If neither foes nor loving friends can hurt you;
    If all men count with you, but none too much;
If you can fill the unforgiving minute
    With sixty seconds' worth of distance run—
Yours is the Earth and everything that's in it,
    And—which is more—you'll be a Man, my son!

Jordan,   AUGUST 13, 2010

As you know this letter comes to you on the cusp of your brother's wedding. It also comes in the midst of a lot of activity ranging from the bachelor party last night to the rehearsal and dinner later today to the ceremony tomorrow. Through it all (and I hope this deeply encourages you) your presence is everywhere.

In fact, given how much your name came up last night at the bachelor party your ears must have been burning. As you well know, after the golfers returned and beers and barbecue were consumed, we did the Hillis thing where everyone gathered around Ryan and shared stories, encouragement, and jokes. With Patrick as master of ceremonies, each of us took a turn. What would have made you feel very good about yourself was the amount of people who, in sharing about Ryan, also ended up saying something about you and the particular relationship that the three of you have together. There was a particular moment where we all raised our drinks and toasted you. It was, to say the least, very moving with a few tears, some laughs, and moments of silence. Stated very succinctly, it was holy.

One of the funniest moments was listening to Patrick tell the story of you and him squaring off to settle, once and for all, who had the better singing voice. He said you two went downstairs, each taking a turn to stand in front of Ryan to sing (of all things) a Christian song ("What if What They Say is True?"[26]) with Ryan being the final judge. The way Patrick finished the story was saying how you both trusted Ryan to

26 Eli Morris, "What If What They Say Is True?" © 1981 CCLI 1956786

give an honest answer. He also noted that you won! You got skillz, boy.

This week (in keeping with all that is happening) I am sending you a line from a poem that for me captures a bit of the poignancy of the time which, simply stated, is my deep wish that you were with us. The line is from a guy by the name of Rainer Maria Rilke where he writes:

Love is this: that two solitudes border, protect, and salute one another.[27]

I want you to deeply, deeply know how much I "salute" who you are as I also try to "protect" and "border" you and what you are becoming.

Your boy, D

---

27 Rainer M. Rilke, *Letters to a Young Poet* (New York: W. W. Norton, 1993), 45.

MISHPACHA REFLECTIONS
Legends
By Pastor Tad Monroe, Friend

It was around a weathered wooden table with Dave Hillis at Engine House No. 9, a pitcher of IPA and two pint glasses between us, that I recall first hearing (in a way of remembering), the words of Jeremiah from the Hebrew scriptures: "But seek the wholeness of the city where I have sent you into exile, and pray to the Lord on its behalf, for in its wholeness you will find your wholeness."[28]

It was around that same table that I began to learn about the Hillis boys—Patrick (P), Ryan (Ry), and Jordan (Jo)—and Dave's philosophy of parenting. It would be a whole other essay to tease out the nuances of that philosophy, but it was grounded in Dave's commitment to expose the boys to the city.

What that produced in the boys more than anything, in my opinion, was a worldview that challenged them to embrace and celebrate paradox, mystery, and the wholeness of individuals and communities.

It would be a few years before I would first meet P, Ry, and Jo, but I got to see this worldview mature in them over the 15 years that followed through our shared life of church, countless family dinners, vacations, basketball and football games, weddings and celebrations, and one-on-one conversations not unlike the ones so formative for me with their father.

---

28 Jeremiah 29:7, NRSVA

P, Ry, and Jo are each *legends* in their own right. But Jordan in particular is the kind of character you'd create for a novel or movie, not the kind of person you actually know. He's the kind of person you tell stories about, and the listener gives you credit for spinning an incredible yarn. But for better or worse, all the credit was due Jordan himself because you weren't exaggerating one bit. But as much of a character as Jordan is, I prefer to think of the boys as a whole. Not because they are not unique, but because their kind of kindred wholeness is the antithesis of dichotomy—individually and collectively. Because their wholeness has a fullness and beauty that is breathtaking and heartbreaking.

If you've ever stepped on a basketball court with the Hillis boys, then you understand this wholeness. Hell, if you've ever been in a gymnasium where even one of them is on the court, even if the others are in the stands, then you understand it.

The wholeness is of course the swagger and absolute fearlessness they share when competing—only eclipsed by the loyalty and trust they have with each other. Three totally different players, choreographed into a nightmare for any opponent willing to step onto the blacktop with them.

P was the point guard with sick handles, a smooth jumper even from downtown, great vision, and the ability to make passes on a dime. His swagger is playful, chirping, with a wink and a smile. He is *Mr. Mayor* on the court and in life—silver-tongued, charming, and more than just a little mischievous.

Ry was the slasher, versatile, and perhaps the best pure athlete (sorry P and Jo). A hard worker with both inside and outside game, fierce defense, and a nice little jumper himself. His swagger is a stoic, quiet, seething intensity—less words and more presence and body language. Thoughtful, demanding, like a potful of passion just at the point of boiling over.

Jo was the enforcer, the muscle, the intimidator. If you weren't already on your heels from P and Ry, then Jo would push you over on your backside (literally and figuratively). Big, long, strong, and very unselfish on the court—doing the little things and the dirty work. His swagger was equally as intense and seething as Ry's, but louder and more verbal. Presence and words that would let you know.

Individually they were different players—if you ever watched them play against each other, it would appear they were trying to hurt each other, unrelenting, and kind of insufferable. But as a squad, either playing together or supporting each other from the stands, what you encountered was an insurmountable wholeness that no other force could stand against.

In every gym across the region, from Enumclaw to Olympia, I watched as their swagger and talent, whether displayed on the court or from the stands, drew the ire of rival opponents and fans alike. I witnessed how they each stepped into the storm as one, leaving no doubt that win or lose, something bigger was at stake than the game being played, any of their individual egos, or statistics. They would hold each other up, defend with fists and words, as we quite literally would have to fight our way out of some of those away game gymnasiums. It didn't matter the consequences, there was no room for words of reason, only a wild and singular brotherhood, a wholeness that displayed each was his brother's keeper no matter the personal cost.

Many of us in Jordan's community were struck by the phrase used by Father Steve Lantry at Jordan's funeral Mass, "Jordan was a complicated grace." This is true and I think, if we are all honest, we know that every (or at least most) grace is complicated.

Jordan was so many things. I could speak to you about his brilliance, his insights, his talents, his work ethic, his determination, his loyalty, his strength and toughness, his faith, his passion, his joy, his humor, his love—all of those things are true. Some might also speak of his myopathy, his poor judgment at times, his lack of impulse control, his inordinate attachments, his rigidness, his pride, his weakness, his despair, his pain, his lack of trust, and his anger—all of those things are also true.

We cannot see clearly if we see these things as contradictions, one thing against another. We can only see clearly (and even then, as through a glass dimly), when we see them as a wholeness where no binary comparison exists, a mysterious whole.

For instance, the way that Jordan was brilliant and insightful could only be forged by the unique relationship between his learning disabilities, his bipolar disorder and Tourette syndrome, his addiction, his pain, his joy, and the people, circumstances, and experiences that shaped and formed him.

Jordan did better than most in holding together the complicated wholeness of individuals, his family, and his community. Though Jordan and I had our impasse moments, to this day I can feel his delight and invitation, as I did at his funeral Mass where I almost audibly heard his voice. As I debated breaking the Catholic Church's (and my own) rule of not taking communion as a non-Catholic I heard him say, *"Tad, come on, get out your seat, take and eat."* And so I did. And I did so with a kind of wholeness that melted away all the dichotomies swirling in my head. I heard his voice again that day, through his brothers, who, despite their own grief, both individually had the same message for me from Jordan, "Tad, he loved you."

What I know is that for those who held Jordan closest, there is a wrestling with the dichotomies even as they know the wholeness better than anyone. Perhaps feeling they failed Jordan somehow, or to feel that Jordan failed them, or to feel that God has failed us all. The insidiousness of this type of dichotomous thinking is that it is the kind of thinking that can allow us to even consider using a word like failure as it relates to Jordan or any of our beloved. It is this kind of thinking that falsely drives us to believe that a *successful* life is a long life, or a life that doesn't involve going to prison, or a life that doesn't include a divorce or a myriad of broken relationships, or a life devoted to playing it safe and avoiding pain at all costs, and so on and so forth.

None of this takes away the sadness and despair for those of us left behind. Perhaps you are one of those parents, siblings, family members, or friends who has loved a complicated soul; who is living the complicated journey of their passing from this life to the next; who is tempted to think that one thing over another *won out* in some sort of black and white battle of good versus bad. But what I believe is that goodness is so big and so whole, that bad is just a footnote, and actually quite relative, and that perhaps what we label as *bad* is the very thing that contributed to the unique goodness of the soul that you loved.

I implore us all not to split our beloved up into a binary that makes it easier for us but diminishes them. Because it will also split us, thinking we somehow could have done one thing or a myriad of other things more perfectly to save them. And that assumes that they needed saving in the first place.

One of Jordan's many tattoos said, "Let the real you, see the real me, holding nothing back." No one I know lived a more authentic life than Jo, and yet still not perfectly authentic. But his story reminds us that no one is ultimately responsible for that life except Jordan and God (or whatever providence you believe in).

Jordan was dealt a hand and he played it. And those who were a part of his community did what they could do to support and celebrate him. I will not for one second see it as a failure, because that would diminish it. It was a complicated life full of complicated grace. It was not easy to embrace all that Jordan was, but it would have been far more tragic to not have received the gift at all. In his wholeness, and our memory of that wholeness, may we find our own.

Jordan, AUGUST 20, 2010

Whereas I usually start out all of my letters to you—"I hope this note finds you well"—I think I will dispense with that salutation because I know it's been a hell-of-a-week for you emotionally, physically, and spiritually. In truth, it's been a hell-of-a-week for me as well. Beginning with the wedding, visiting you on Saturday and seeing the tough place you were in, and then having to figure out my own emotions—all produced a difficult week.

It is times like this that lead me to deeply question the God who I have given my life to. I often wonder why things take place the way they do. Where is the peace that we all so long for? Why is it that some people seem to get ahead while others don't? I share these raw emotions with you Jo to give you some sense (and I hope this is encouraging to you) that you are not in your pain alone.

Interestingly enough, while I was fighting with my emotions I began to sense that one of the things that God was asking me to do was "carry your burdens"[29] (which is a verse in the Bible). Upon sensing that, I texted Mark and Mike on Tuesday and asked them "if they would be willing to pray with me that God give us your burdens, thus lightening your load." They, of course, both readily agreed. I will be interested to talk with you to see if you sensed that "your burden" this week felt any lighter. If so, maybe this prayer-shit really works!

---

29 Galatians 6:2

Speaking of praying for others, you can be praying for your boy, Patrick. I had a very hard conversation with him recently. While talking with him it became very obvious that leaving for Ireland so soon, him and Teresa's relationship, and his overall tiredness is making him very sad as well.

I don't have much poetry in me this week—sorry about that. Or maybe another way to say it is my poetry to you this week is simply this: I love you and am very proud to be your father.

Your boy, D

Jordan,

I hope this letter finds you well. I heard a bit from your brothers when they visited you last week as well as about some of your phone calls. All in all it sounds as though things have gotten a bit easier and better since Whitney and I saw you. I am glad to hear it.

I just returned from a trip to Texas where it was 104, 105, and 102 degrees the three days I was there. It was the closest thing to Thailand I have ever felt, but our trip is still on top. Do you remember how hot it was? I still remember that night in Bangkok when we returned to our room and found that the air conditioning hadn't been turned on. We were both miserable for a while!

By the time you get this letter Mark, Cheryl, and I will have seen you (Sunday morning). We are all looking forward to the trip, but your Aunt Cheryl is in particular. As you well know, all of your family deeply cares about you, but your aunt has a special regard for you.

I don't know if you have heard, but Patrick and Teresa made it to Ireland and have also been able to find a place with two bedrooms. I hear it is within walking distance to his school and a number of nice pubs. I am sure Patrick will get very familiar with many of those bartenders!

In the spirit of Patrick and Teresa being in Ireland, I thought I would send you one of my favorite Irish poets. As you know, Ireland has many famous poets (Wilde, Lewis, etc.), but the one I have enjoyed most is W.B. Yeats. I am sending you his poem "The Second Coming," where he writes about his notion of Jesus returning. One of the reasons I like the poem is its description of life: "The ceremony of innocence is drowned; The best lack all conviction, while the worst are full of passionate intensity." I don't know about you but this is often the way I feel on the streets of Tacoma and other cities I travel in. Little kids are not allowed to be kids anymore and as a result their "innocence is drowned"; people who could do something good and make changes "lack all conviction"; and finally the ones that are messing shit up are "full of passionate intensity" where they make all the noise. Is this your take? Let me know what you think about the poem.

As always, Jo, I send my deep love for you and I am looking forward to seeing you tomorrow.

Your boy, D

The Second Coming
By William Butler Yeats

Turning and turning in the widening gyre
The falcon cannot hear the falconer;
Things fall apart; the centre cannot hold;
Mere anarchy is loosed upon the world,
The blood-dimmed tide is loosed, and everywhere
The ceremony of innocence is drowned;
The best lack all conviction, while the worst
Are full of passionate intensity.

Surely some revelation is at hand;
Surely the Second Coming is at hand.
The Second Coming! Hardly are those words out
When a vast image out of *Spiritus Mundi*
Troubles my sight: somewhere in sands of the desert
A shape with lion body and the head of a man,
A gaze blank and pitiless as the sun,
Is moving its slow thighs, while all about it
Reel shadows of the indignant desert birds.
The darkness drops again; but now I know
That twenty centuries of stony sleep
Were vexed to nightmare by a rocking cradle,
And what rough beast, its hour come round at last,
Slouches towards Bethlehem to be born?

FALL

Jordan,

I am writing to you at the end of what feels like a very long week. I suppose you have had more than your fair share of this! Suffice it to say when I experience one of these weeks my esteem (which I didn't think could get any higher) grows even more for you given your ability to get through them with your integrity intact and your hope still growing.

I am looking forward to the Labor Day weekend. I need some time to rest, do some reading, workout, and drink some wine. I also—and here you can pray for me—am going to try and quit smoking starting Tuesday. My sense is that as I get older I probably have less of a safety net to play around with than I used to have.

I know I speak for all of us when I say how much we enjoyed the time with you last weekend. Everybody commented to me on how good you seem, the strength that you exude, and the very positive outlook you have. Every one of us walked away from the time hoping we could be a bit more like you (minus the bars).

Chase's first game is tonight against your old rival—the Wilson Rams. Although the paper picked Stadium last (for the umpteenth time) in the league, Tad and the other coaches are cautiously optimistic. Tonight is a very big game for them in regards to their self-confidence. I am deeply hoping that Chase will have a great game where he catches a few balls and maybe gets a pick or two on the defensive side.

I don't have a poem I am sending your way, but do have a Martin Luther King Jr. reflection that I actually keep framed on my office wall. He wrote:

> *Rarely do we find men who willingly engage in hard, solid thinking. There is an almost universal quest for easy answers and half-baked solutions. Nothing pains some people more than having to think.*[30]

I want you to know that you are one of the few people who I see living out Dr. King's truth. You have a fearless tenacity to ask hard questions and live with difficult answers. My sense is this has served you well. I know it has served me well.

I hope we can talk this weekend.

Your boy, D

---

30 Dr. Martin Luther King, "A Tough Mind and a Tender Heart," in *Strength to Love* (Philadelphia: Fortress, 2010), 13.

MISHPACHA REFLECTIONS
JD
By Mark Hillis, Uncle

I was intimidated when Cheryl (a.k.a. Sugar or Sug) and I found out that we were going to have our first child. My brother, Dave, and his wife, Teresa, already had three boys with large personalities. I knew that my kid was going to have to find a way to get a word in—it wasn't going to be handed to him.

JD was born in 1986. He was our first of four boys and 18 months younger than Jordan. To my surprise, it quickly became clear that my fears of JD trying to get a word in edgewise wasn't going to be an issue. He was graciously welcomed by his three older cousins: Patrick, Ryan, and Jordan. Being older, Patrick and Ryan were often busy testing life and had other interests as well. This meant that JD and Jordan spent much more time together and became best friends. A deep bond was formed—it was the start of a grace that lasted eight and a half years. JD loved all his cousins but Jo was special. A description of Jo that I had heard recently was that he "loved fiercely." It couldn't have been more true in light of his relationship with JD. On numerous occasions, Jo came to JD's aid. Whether it was confronting a kid that stole JD's ball or encouraging JD to mix it up in games, Jo was there. Their personalities weren't cut from the same cloth. JD was a follower who believed that *no* actually meant *no*—Jo thought no was an opportunity. This dynamic of their personalities played well with each other. Through Jo's 'yeah, I can do that' attitude, JD learned to step out when everything in him told him not to. The result was that they played on baseball and soccer teams together, and played a lot of basketball. Conversely, JD was a calming influence on Jo. One of the consequences of 'large personalities' was an occasional fight between the cousins. But when JD showed up, the fight was over. He and Jo would find something to do that required no brothers and no parents. Jo was the big brother that JD thought he was meant to have.

JD passed away on March 13th, 1995 from an AVM (arteriovenous malformation). Just a couple of days before, he had spent the night at Jordan's house for Jo's 10th birthday. I am still thankful for that.

One of my fears after JD had passed was that my boys—Cory, Chase, and Matt—would feel disconnected from their older cousins. JD was an important link between them all. It was a hard time and I saw how especially hard it was on Jordan. Occasionally, he and I would talk a little bit about losing JD. It was infrequent but heartfelt. It was a little awkward at first but Jo had always had a high view of family. And I think because of that, not to engage with his younger cousins wasn't an option. Needless to say, my boys ate up the attention. Jo didn't (nor wouldn't) replace JD but he did everything within his power to bridge that gap.

Our youngest, Matt, was born after JD had passed. Even though Jo was 14 years older than Matt, he kind of took him under his wing and taught Matt things about working out. He helped Matt set up a boxing ring in the basement and then proceeded to show Matt what *exactly* a boxing workout looked like. Matt would also run the bowl with Jo, who would pick him up at 5 a.m.—a workout ethic that Matt has never forgotten.

Chase, eight years younger than Jo, remembers the times when Jo would hype him up. During Cory and Alia's wedding, for example, Chase was anxious about having to speak. Sensing this, Jo came up to Chase with a healthy drink in hand, handed it to him, spanked him on the ass and said, "You got this boy." As Chase would say, Jo was the first to hand dap him as he came into a room.

Although all of the boys' relationships with Jo were heartfelt, Jo's relationship with Cory was different—maybe because of Cory's relationship with JD. Cory has claimed that his love for boxing came directly from Jo. It became a regular occurrence that Jo and Cor would check in with each other any time a big fight was about to happen. Another story that thankfully I only heard about secondhand was a Fourth of July gathering a number of years ago. Generally, Cor wanted to make the rounds with his friends, but he got a call from Jo asking to hang out. Jo took him to a party that Cory said 'was the most unsafe and safe time' he'd felt in his life. Sensing that a 'fight could pop off at any moment,' Cor also knew that he was with Jo. And all was good.

This was Jordan. One of the most incarnational people I've ever been around. Life was meant to be lived. And it was his intent to make sure the boys lived life with intent. He engaged with them. He encouraged them. He pushed them. But Jo wouldn't play. He held the boys to a high bar. Whether it was his sense of duty or because he felt a responsibility to JD to take care of the boys, I don't know. If they were taking the easy path, Jo would call them on it. And then just as quickly, grace them as one who understood that life wasn't about being good—it was about giving and receiving mercy.

A Grace that both Sug and I were given was when Jordan and Tiffany had their first child, Jimmy David Hillis, named for his two grandfathers, Jimmy McHenry and my brother Dave. Jo sat down with Sug and I and asked if it would be alright to name his boy JD and if we would be his godparents. Knowing that my response wouldn't reflect how much that meant to me, I hugged him. But that was Jo—always thinking of family. For Sug and I, we watched so much of this: Jo interacting with JD, Cory, Chase, and Matt. We all felt that we were in Jo's world. And with Jo, when you are in, you're in. Jo and JD were certainly the catalysts that started this relationship with our family, but Jo moved it to a depth that we have been the fortunate recipients of, and we have tried, in our own way, to do likewise.

Jo,   SEPTEMBER 10, 2010

Greetings my young brother! I hope this week has come and gone quickly for you. I know that one of your prayers is that this time would move quickly. It may be encouraging to you that this is already my 22nd letter to you (which doesn't include those first few weeks in County) which means time is moving at a pretty good clip. Before you know it, you will be out and back with us.

I have continued to work my way through the book on the Mafia. I may have mentioned this already, but I am intrigued that the word itself means "our thing." I don't know about you, but it often seems to me that those things that are most important to us are also the ones that can be hardest to define. For example, when you think about what takes place at Hillis family gatherings it would be hard to define precisely what it is that brings us together. Certainly we would say family (but of course there are a lot of families that don't come together), food, friendship, laughter, etc. But in the end we might, similar to the Mafia, need to say something like "we come together because it is 'our thing'." Interesting!

On another Mafia note, I have definitely decided that Carlo Gambino is my favorite. If it can actually be said in such a way, he did organized crime with style and character. I like the fact that he seems to have never lost his temper, he would walk down the streets of Brooklyn to stay in touch with the common people, that he and his wife never created a mansion like some of the other bosses, etc.

This week I am sending you a very simple little poem by Mary Oliver called "The Uses of Sorrow." It is one of those poems that at first glance can seem so simple that you find yourself saying, "What's the big deal?" But you'll notice the first two lines ("Someone I loved once gave me a box full of darkness") have no punctuation (period, comma, colon, etc.). What this allows for you to do is decide whether you say:

"Someone I loved, once gave me a box full of darkness" (where the emphasis is on a person who I still currently love), or "Someone I loved once, gave me a box full of darkness" (where the emphasis is on a person I used to love, but not anymore).

It's kind of interesting, is it not?

Alright, enough literary stuff for now. I hope to talk or see you soon.

Your boy, D

Uses of Sorrow
By Mary Oliver

Someone I loved once gave me
a box full of darkness.

It took me years to understand
that this, too, was a gift.

Jo,

It's another Friday (they seem to be coming very fast) and as a result it's time for me to sit down and scribble out a note to you. I trust that this note will find you well.

I wanted to begin by saying that Mom told me you are praying for me about our application for government grants and my smoking. Thank you very much. Your willingness to do this for me makes me feel deeply loved by you in that you would find the time and energy to offer such a prayer. It becomes even more important in that I am in a very difficult place emotionally, where I have had deep questions about whether I am doing a very good job of leading Leadership Foundations. That sense of failure and living with it has never been a very strong Hillis trait. It has also raised some very significant questions about my relationship with God. Things like, would God call me to this Leadership Foundations job and have me fail? Why has God (as of today) not met the financial needs of the organization I am responsible for leading? Does God's activity or lack of activity have anything to do with all of the things I have done wrong? And if that is true, why will God not forgive me? It is in the midst of these questions (and there are many more if you ever want to hear about them all) that your prayers mean so much to me. I am, to put it mildly, a very fragile man. I suppose that this is what Oscar Wilde must have meant when he wrote, "all men are in the gutter; but some look up at the stars."[31] Your prayers are helping me look up at the stars!

---

31 Oscar Wilde, "Lady Windermere's Fan," in *Oscar Wilde Play Collection: The Importance of Being Earnest, Lady Windermere's Fan, a Woman of No Importance, an Ideal Husband.* (N.p.: Independently Published, 2020).

The poem I am sending you is another Mary, titled "Whispered Poem." I like this one because it is so short and so much reminds me of you. She writes:

> *I have been risky in my endeavors,*
> *I have been steadfast in my loves;*
> *Oh Lord, consider these when you judge me.*

Don't you think this is so true of you? You have been risky as hell and I so admire what you have done and the way you have done it. You have also remained absolutely true to your family, friends, and commitments. As a result Jo, when your opportunity comes to meet the great God of the universe that we know in the person of Jesus, I think it will go very well for you. Your risk and your steadfastness are marks of the Holy Spirit in you and I have gleaned much. Truth be told, you are a model for me in these two areas.

As always, much love.

D

Jordan,

I hope you are well. I have continued to think and meditate all week on how much I enjoyed my time with you last Sunday. In truth, it was both the highlight of my week and, as a result, something that I continued to use as a major source of energy in the midst of some very difficult circumstances.

Maybe more importantly—and you might find this comment a bit curious—you have become an anchor for me. I don't know if I can explain it very well or, for that matter, if I even understand it. But somehow the way that you are dealing with your situation through your regimented workouts, commitment to honesty, discipline in reading, willingness to make amends, all have had the net effect of giving me hope that good things can happen. Maybe stated another way, your time at McNeil has become my own *Shawshank Redemption*, where you are modeling for me what it means to "come out clean on the other side."[32] So thanks, my young brother.

I am sending you another poem from Mary this week. It is from her latest book, *Swan*, and the poem is called "The Poet is Told to Fill Up More Pages." There are a number of reasons this poem appeals to me, but let me name three. The first is that she starts with what I think is a very honest assessment ("But, where are the words?"). I don't know about you, but I so often find myself in situations where the very thing I need does not seem to be readily available. Whether this has been in how to love your mother through some of her health issues, trying

---

32 Frank Darabont, dir. *The Shawshank Redemption*. CA: Warner Brothers, 1994.

to be a father to you and your brothers, or leading Leadership Foundations—all seem to ask something of me that I often feel I don't have. The second thing she does is describe how she does try to do something ("For fun I try a few commands myself... Nothing happens"), but to no effect. This too has been my reality. If I could ever tell you all of the things I have tried to do (play the Lotto, make promises to God that if God gives me what I need I will never do that again, etc.) you would shit on yourself from laughing so hard. The third (and this is the hopeful part) is that she finally decides that all she can do is make herself available ("All I can give you, not being the maker of what I do, but only the one that holds the pencil"). It is this "availability" that I am hoping to get better at. It is also this "availability" that you have taught me about.

Your very thankful father,

D

The Poet is Told to Fill Up More Pages
By Mary Oliver

But, where are the words?
Not in my pocket.
Not in the refrigerator.
Not in my savings account.

So I sit, harassed, with my notebook.
It's a joke, really, and not a good one.
For fun I try a few commands myself.
I say to the rain, stop raining.
I say to the sun, that isn't anywhere nearby,
Come back, and come fast.

Nothing happens.

So this is all I can give you,
not being the maker of what I do,
but only the one that holds the pencil.

abcdefghijklmnopqrstuvwxyz.
Make of it what you will.

MISHPACHA REFLECTIONS
Comfortable Silence
By Tyler Hillis, Cousin

With the three brothers Dave, Mark, and Mike all having kids and living in the same city it should come as no surprise that those kids became more than just extended family. They became brothers and sisters to one another in that mysterious way love works sometimes.

I was the only one of the next generation of Hillis' with no *immediate brother*. JD, Cor, Chase, and Matt all had each other. And Pack, Ry, and Jo did too. My sister had me. And so for a while growing up, I was bitter about this fact. I worried I was missing out on some great experience that everyone else was having. But, with age I realized I wasn't missing anything—I was fortunate to have so many cousins that had transcended typical definition.

Jo was the one that finally made me realize it. He was one of the "big three" in my mind. Those older cousins had an aura of greatness—each with something unique and awe-inspiring. For Jo, it was his unexpected warmth and vulnerability even with such a tough exterior. If you were to walk into a room full of Hillis' (perhaps an intimidating thing to do due to the overwhelming volume of voices trying to speak over one another), Jo had a knack for finding the spaces that were slightly disconnected from the rest—out in front of the house in a patio chair, in the kitchen preparing steak, or by the fire pit before the cigars had arrived. For the unfamiliar, a lean, muscular, tattooed man wearing a beanie, white tank-top undershirt, and some sweatpants off by himself might not be the first person you'd go up to.

But for me, Jo was always my first stop. Because as soon as he saw you approach, his resting grimace melted into a smile that was as welcoming as his deep hugs, or his huge hands as he dapped you up (he always snapped his fingers after). He was the tone-setter for the gathering of family—a flourishing upstroke of a conductor starting a wonderful symphony.

During my second year of college I had a close friend commit suicide. It was an event so profoundly sad that I found it hard to find any joy for a long while. We had a family gathering while I was going through this experience. But this time, I chose to distance myself from the cacophony of human noise—preferring a bit of solitude. And, thankfully, the family understood where I was at and let me be.

But, unusually, I hadn't sought after Jo on my arrival. I can't speak for why exactly Jo came looking for me—perhaps he had noted my lack of greeting, or maybe he saw me distanced, like he so often could be, and understood that sometimes those apart are the most in need of something. Whatever the reason, Jo came looking.

When he found me—no doubt disengaged and staring into that middle distance where sadness looms—he sat next to me. He wore no grimace, no warm smile, but a simple face of open understanding. He said, "I heard about your friend Jake. I'm here for you, bro."

I knew he had been through hard times. I knew he had lost

friends in the same way I had. I had never seen him struggle in the same way I was at that time but his words spoke to that vulnerability. It was jarring coming from him.

We sat there for a while, in comfortable silence, thinking about the friends and family we had lost. It's only in retrospect that I know this was when I started to realize I'd had brothers my entire life. I may have been jealous of the biological definition, but what all of us cousins had was much deeper than that. Much deeper than what most other people have the opportunity to experience. And I will forever thank Jo for being my brother.

When Jo passed I felt that same profound sadness I had before. But, this time, when the family gathered, Jo was not there to come looking. And, I'm sure, all anyone in the Hillis family wanted to do was to simply sit with him in comfortable silence for a while.

So, since Jo didn't come looking, I went looking for him. When grief was swallowing me up, I was able to find an inkling of our connection by writing a letter in the immediate aftermath. It was the closest thing I had to saying goodbye to one of my brothers. And after I was done, it felt as if we were back on that couch, sitting next to one another, thinking about the friends and family we had lost.

Jordan, OCTOBER 1, 2010

Well, can you believe it? I am writing to you on the first day of October. Your time at McNeil is going to be over before you know it! That will be a very sweet time indeed.

This letter is going to be rather short. I am knee-deep in preparing to fly out to Cincinnati for the week tomorrow. It is where the LF Training Institute (all the local Leadership Foundations meet for three days to receive training) and board meeting (my bosses) will take place. By the time you receive this (usually Tuesday) I will be in the midst of it all. I would deeply appreciate your prayers for two things: that all of my speaking responsibilities go well and that we will get some good news in the next few days about finances so I can give the board a good report. Without hearing any good news, I am afraid the meeting with my board may be rather tough.

I did finish the book on the Mafia and have started *Pound for Pound*. As to the book on the Mafia I am glad I read it and have a lot of respect for Carlo Gambino, but Gotti, from my estimation, is a serious punk. I kept waiting to read something redeemable about the guy, but nothing ever surfaced. I suppose (assuming it is true) that reading about what he did to that guy who inadvertently killed his kid in a car accident colored my perception. That act seems to me to be very cowardly, particularly when the guy came to the Gotti house to ask for their forgiveness. Regarding *Pound for Pound* (I am about a quarter of the way through), I have two initial thoughts. The first is that I don't find myself liking Sugar very much. Do you have that feeling? There is no doubt about his skill as a boxer, but his person is unappealing compared to someone like Dempsey. My other initial thought is I am not sure I like the way the author writes. Whereas the guy who wrote about Dempsey made the story come alive, this person feels removed and dispassionate. I will keep reading, but am already anticipating the next book you will recommend to me. If I remember correctly you think the LaMotta story was a good one. Am I correct?

By way of a poem this week I am sending you one in celebration of your mom and I's 30th wedding anniversary that took place this past week. It is by Robert Bly and it is called "A Third Body." I like it for a number of reasons, but two of the reasons in particular capture our relationship. The first is the way he describes how they have learned to be content. I think your mom and I have finally learned this valuable lesson. The second is that any good marriage actually creates ("Third Body"). Stated another way, part of the beauty (and the difficulty) of marriage is that you can't just focus on yourself, but what you are giving away to this world. This, too, is something I am very thankful for with your mother: I think in our own small way we have created for others. At least I hope so.

Finally, my letter next week will come late. I don't get back to T-Town until Friday night. I will write you first thing Saturday morning.

Your boy, D

A Third Body
By Robert Bly
From *Loving a Woman in Two Worlds*

A man and a woman sit near each other,

and they do not long at this moment to be older, or younger,

nor born in any other nation, or time, or place.

They are content to be where they are, talking or not talking.

Their breaths together feed someone whom we do not know.

The man sees the way his fingers move;

he sees her hands close around a book she hands to him.

They obey a third body that they share in common.

They have made a promise to love that body.

Age may come, parting may come, death will come.

A man and a woman sit near each other;

as they breathe they feed someone we do not know,

someone we know of, whom we have never seen.

Jo,   OCTOBER 8, 2010

It is Monday morning and I am still feeling the power of our time together yesterday. I have attempted to try to come to grips with our meeting through an effort at some language to describe the time—nothing so far. If I did have to hazard a guess at this point it would be the word *Holy*. Not Holy in the way that we usually think about the term (moral, pure, without sin, etc.), but how it was demonstrated in Jesus. In essence, holiness in Jesus is someone who does not judge, is transparent with their struggle, and celebrates others. In all of these ways (and many more) you blessed me with your holiness.

Regarding our conversation, I wanted to mention two things. The first is the verse I quoted to you about there being "no condemnation in Christ Jesus."[33] I have included all of the verses, but have found that this is one of the most powerful statements I know and one I sense you are struggling with and seeking to find an answer around. But can you imagine, Jo—NO CONDEMNATION! In the midst of a world that is always seeking to condemn, make fun of, ridicule, dis, punk, etc., in Jesus there is none of that. Which leads to the second thing: you and Jesus.

You asked "how it happens." In many ways I would say it has been happening to you for a long time, of which you are beginning to recognize. There are as many different ways to say 'yes' to Jesus (become a Christian) as there are people in this world. To that end, I am including a prayer that has been used

---

33 Romans 1:8

by others to signify their commitment to Jesus. In some ways it becomes a kind of birthday whereby this becomes the day you consciously said 'yes.' It might be great to take this prayer and go to the chapel and simply read it out loud to God.

Finally, I am sending you another poem. This one is by Denise Levertov about another poet whose name is Rainer Maria Rilke. Rilke was a very complex guy who did some very ugly stuff, but in the end became open to God. The reason I am sending it to you is the last line. In listening to you describe your experience in the chapel (which I can tell you how absolutely thrilling it was to listen to) it reminded of this line: "The day's blow rang out, metallic—or it was I, a bell awakened, and what I heard was my whole self saying and singing what it knew: I can."

My sense, my dear boy, is that something took place in you in that chapel where "a bell awakened" and that the result is that you are beginning to sense "you can," which is the most freeing and exhilarating reality there is.

All of this continues to move me to tell you how very fortunate I feel I am to be in this with you. Simply stated, I am being given the great chance to see the sweetness of God work again and again.

I love you and will see you next weekend.

Your boy, D

Variation on a Theme by Rilke
By Denise Levertov

A certain day became a presence to me;
there it was, confronting me—a sky, air, light:
a being. And before it started to descend
from the height of noon, it leaned over
and struck my shoulder as if with
the flat of a sword, granting me
honor and a task. The day's blow
rang out, metallic—or it was I, a bell awakened,
and what I heard was my whole self
saying and singing what it knew: I can.

Jordan,

I am sitting in my office waiting for a phone call so I decided to take the time to write my Friday letter to you.

It has been quite a week for a number of reasons. One of those reasons is being gone last week. Being away from my office as long as I was results in me walking back into a whole host of emails and phone calls. So much so that it makes me wish I had never left my office in the first place. The other reason that surfaced is that my board decided that my team and I have four months to figure out how the Leadership Foundations office is going to operate financially. If we don't, the board is going to close the office down and I will be out of a job. Who knows, maybe you and I will be looking for a job together! I got your back if you got mine. I have also, along with those reasons, been thinking a lot about you.

To start with, I quit smoking on Monday as I told you I would. Along with it being better for me I am also using it to remind myself to ask God to allow me to help carry your burdens. Already this week when I have been tempted to smoke I immediately thought about you and found myself able to get through the lure of having a smoke. I wanted to let you know that, in part because I am hoping that in me asking for your burden you have felt lighter this week, but also because your predicament is helping me become healthier. Go figure. I also have been thinking a great deal about you as it relates to whether the prayer I sent you was of any help. Was it? It is very important for me to have you know that while the prayer I sent you can be helpful, what is most important to God is your authentic voice that simply cries out for God's presence. As a result there is no formula for saying yes to the magnetic and overwhelming personality of Jesus, but simply a result of seeing him for who he is (mercy incarnated) and kneeling to that power. Ironically, one of the best examples of this process is what you and I have talked about as it relates to the Mafia. As you know better than anyone, when they are inducted in and made a "fellah" there is no great ceremony, but a simple acknowledgement of the code. This is what it looks like to be a Christian—a simple acknowledgement of the code. The only difference being that the code in the case of Christianity is the person of Jesus. I hope this makes sense.

It is in light of all this that I am sending you a poem that speaks to what it means to 'become a Christian' or 'born again.' The poet's name is George MacDonald. He was a Scotsman who lived in the 1800s and whom C.S. Lewis considered his spiritual mentor. I like this poem a lot because it describes the experience you are going through in real terms—not something that is out of Hollywood. He begins by saying (which you and I both know is true), "tis hard to rouse our spirits up." I think this captures a big part of what has been going on with you and is so difficult, that, as MacDonald states, "many will rather lie among the slain." But for those who want to move on like you, they "urge ourselves to life with holy greed." This has been my prayer for you of late, Jo: to urge yourself on with "holy greed."

Much love and I look forward to seeing you Sunday. D

Diary of an Old Soul
By George MacDonald

Tis hard for us to rouse our spirits up—
It is the human creative agony
Though but to hold the heart an empty cup
Or tighten on the team the rigid reign.
Many will rather lie among the slain
Than creep through narrow ways the light to gain—
Than wake the will, and be born bitterly.

But we who would be born again indeed,
Must wake our souls unnumbered times a day
And urge ourselves to life with holy greed.
Now open our bosoms to the wind's free play,
And now, with patience forceful, hard, lie still
Submiss and ready to the making will,
Athirst and empty, for God's breath to fill.

MISHPACHA REFLECTIONS
It's All Love
By Lina Thompson, Friend

I met Jordan and his brothers Ryan and Patrick when I moved to Tacoma in 1987 to work for Young Life, a faith-based youth program. Jordan was two.

I spent a lot of time around the Hillis family in those years. Watching them grow up, I will be honest, it was interesting to see how these three moved in the Tacoma community as white kids from a middle-class family. All three learned what it means to be good friends with all kinds of people. They attended public schools even when they had the opportunity for private education, which said a lot to me about their love for the city. They hooped almost all the time, so much so that they put in a legit basketball court in their backyard and it became the spot for all their friends. I loved being around them. There was always a flurry of activity in their home.

Some days I would bring high school kids over to play basketball. It was another place for our kids to be safe and out of trouble. Even though the kids I brought were much older than the Hillis boys, it didn't matter. Community is like that: All are welcome. Meaningful relationships were forged in these ways over many, many years, producing deep respect. As the kids say, *it's all love*.

Jordan was always in the mix—good and bad—at school or at his home away from home, the Al Davies Boys and Girls Club. He spent time coming to our learning center to get help every day with homework. I loved seeing him there, working with high school tutors that were the same ones who would show up later to hoop in his backyard!

That way of "community" raised and shaped Jordan and he stayed true to it. Jordan loved Tacoma. And Tacoma, embodied in these relationships, loved him back for 30+ years.

That kind of love is a powerful force. A spiritual one too. As a pastor, I have learned to pay attention to these things. Said another way, I am interested in how the Spirit moves in the world and want to pay attention to the signs that bear witness to God's activity. I'm not always sure I see it, but I have tried to train my eyes to look for signs of grace.

Someone offered this image of grace, and it has helped me: "Grace is like water. It flows downhill and pools up in the lowest places."

Talk about a complicated grace. It suggests that we see and experience the fullness of this grace and all its beauty when we journey to the lowest places in our own lives and in the lives of others. I will admit, as great as grace is, I'm not sure if I would choose to go there—to the low places. It takes courage and a love for people. I saw this grace in Jordan. He gravitated toward those "low places." He had an authentic compassion for those who were suffering. Jordan's first move was toward, not away. He had an intuition about this way of grace, and he trusted it. I wonder if he trusted it more for others than maybe he did for himself. We all struggle with that.

It's the kind of grace that shows up for people, no matter what. I saw this firsthand in a relationship Jordan had with two of those kids who spent time in the Hillis' backyard all those years ago. Like Jordan, they suffered their own personal battles with addiction. And they, too, have an incredible capacity for walking in grace with and for others. I was surprised (and not) when I found out the three of them were locked up in County at the same time (all unrelated experiences). It was a sweet reunion, as you can probably imagine. I loved hearing them tell that story.

Jordan showed up for them while they were locked up and then also when they were out. He kept up with them. He checked in on them. They were crushed to hear of Jordan's passing as they had so much respect for him. *It's all love.*

Being in solidarity with those who suffer and reminding people that they are seen, loved, and not forgotten—these were the gifts of Jordan's life. I saw that. Even writing about it makes me weepy to know that this Gift of a life, this Grace, isn't here any longer.

If the Christian journey is about maturing our ability to "see" that movement of grace to the low places, Jordan's life was more mature than a lot of people who sit in pews every week. He was not perfect and he didn't pretend to be. He endured suffering. He had his own battles he was fighting. I don't get how it works, but that imperfection and suffering shapes us in ways that create capacity to be a beautiful, gracious presence in the world, however complicated.

Jordan,

I hope you are well. It was great to talk with you the other night and I am looking forward to what will be our weekly calls each Thursday night from here until the time you get out.

I want to begin this letter by thanking you for the honest conversation we had on the phone. I am very proud that you are beginning to understand how courageous one must be in order to admit they are weak. It is ironic, isn't it? As you and I have talked, most of the people who are in serious trouble—whether with the law, family, friends, finances, etc.—are in that situation because they were not courageous enough to admit they were afraid. The strongest people I know are those who are aware of how weak they are. Interestingly (and this is the poem I am sending you this week), one of the things I do for you and your brothers is pray a particular prayer for you each day. One of the lines in the prayer is "Lord, build me a son who is strong enough to know when he is weak; brave enough to face himself when he is afraid." So you see, in coming to a place of understanding how the particular job you had is not working and being willing to admit it, you have given me an answer to my prayer. Well done.

The other thing I want to thank you for is turning me on to the book about Teddy Atlas. Along with it being very well written, it is also remarkably similar to your own story. Whether it was the way that Teddy first got into trouble (being willing to do anything and not caring about the ramifications), his slow recognition of his own insecurities, his dying to his dream of being a boxer because of his neck condition, all have reminded me of you which has been very enjoyable. I also love some of the other characters. Cus appears to be a remarkable man. I love the way he thinks about boxing as a metaphor for life. I also enjoy the Catholic priest.

Finally, the poem this week is called "Prayer for a Son" by General Douglas MacArthur. You may be more familiar with this than you think. This poem is framed around pictures of you, Ryan, and Patrick. Do you remember it? I ran across this many years ago when you three were very young, thought it was perfect, and have used it as my daily prayer for each of you. There are so many things I like about it. As mentioned earlier, I like the fact that it prays for what I would call 'counterintuitive realities'. For example, it is easy to pray for things like "make my children successful, rich, happy, etc." but honestly who cares about that. It is nice if they come, but I want something bigger and deeper for you. I also like the idea built into the poem that your whole sense of becoming is a process. It does not happen immediately or overnight. The third thing I like is that it acknowledges the inherent tensions in life. For example, "mastering yourself before you master others," and, "always be serious, but not take himself too seriously." Finally, I like the way it ties you and I together—as you become these things I will realize that I "have not lived in vain."

Regarding this last one, I want you to know how much of an answer to this prayer you have already become and, as a result, you have allowed me to realize I have not lived in vain.

Thanks, Jo. Your boy, D.

Prayer for a Son[34]
By General Douglas MacArthur

Build me a son, O Lord, who will be strong enough to know when he is weak, and brave enough to face himself when he is afraid; one who will be proud and unbending in honest defeat, and humble and gentle in victory.

Build me a son whose wishes will not take the place of deeds; a son who will know Thee—and that it is the foundation stone of knowledge.

Lead him I pray, not in the path of ease and comfort, but under the stress and spur of difficulties and challenge. Here let him learn to stand up in the storm; here let him learn compassion for those who fail.

Build me a son whose heart will be clean, whose goal will be high; a son who will master himself before he seeks to master other men; one who will reach into the future, yet never forget the past.

And after all these things are his, add, I pray, enough of a sense of humor, so that he may always be serious, yet never take himself too seriously.

Give him humility, so that he may always remember the simplicity of true greatness, the open mind of true wisdom, the meekness of true strength.

Then, I, his father, will dare to whisper, "I have not lived in vain."

---

34 Douglas MacArthur, *Reminiscences* (N.p.: Naval Institute Press, 2001).

Jo,

It is Friday morning and I am here at my office early trying to get some things done before your mom, Ry, Kasi, and I hit the road. I am looking forward to tasting some wine with your boy.

Thanks for the conversation last night. It is always good to chop it up with you. You are a great conversationalist. I think this is principally due to your willingness to speak the truth, your wide breadth of knowledge, and your ability to see humor in things that are often not apparent to the naked eye. All are great gifts that I see growing in their scope and span. It continues to give me a deep confidence that there is a "greatness" that awaits you as you continue to make those hard, difficult, lonely, decisions in the deep places of your life.

It is this last thought—you making decisions in those deep places—that reminded me of a poem that I should have sent you much earlier for a number of reasons. The first is that it was a poem (maybe more accurately **the** poem) that allowed Nelson Mandela to survive 27 years in prison in South Africa. I know how much you respect him. Second, the poem captures a number of themes that have been important to you through the years. The first is the poem's brutally honest opening line "Out of the night that covers me," which of course is not just the physical night, but the darkness that surrounds us all. Immediately the poet thanks "whatever gods may be" for this darkness. And while I, of course, would not just thank the gods, but Jesus, the premise holds true: The key to an "unconquerable soul" is thankfulness. Not strength (although that is nice), or natural gifts (another nice thing), or even family and friends (very necessary), but thankfulness for all of those things.

In the second stanza, he writes, "in the fell clutch of circumstance" which I take as a way of saying we are all products of things that we cannot control. I think this is one of the single hardest things to learn: how to live life when you have been given a shit-storm to live with. I will never be able to adequately explain to you why your best friend was taken from you. Neither will I be able to clarify why you have the burden of dyslexia and Tourette syndrome. But what I can tell you—which people like Mandela, so many of the boxers you admire, and even some of the Mafia exemplify—is that while your "head is bloody" it can be "unbowed." My sense is that this is not a prideful posture as much as not giving in to the shame and regret that nips at all of our souls.

The third stanza is wonderful as well. Again, in a very honest and transparent way, the poet notes that he abides "Beyond this place of wrath and tears, looms but the horror of the shade," which is to say that the work God is doing in us does not eliminate these things that we find so difficult (although we very much wish it were so), but works in and through them ("looms the horror of shade"). You know this truth well—no quick fixes.

And of course the final stanza may be one of the best in all of English literature. In light of our conversations around a number of things I think of how poignant the line "It matters not how strait the gate, How charged with punishments the scroll," must be to you. The poet has the wisdom to know that all of us are haunted by the idea that if God and others knew the shit I did they would never forgive me. Yet he knows, as you are also realizing, that those things can be vanquished and completely neutralized if we take responsibility and operate as individuals that believe "I am the master of my fate. I am the captain of my soul."

A final word: Mandela reports that he read this poem every day he was in prison and that it had a lot to do with his survival. I am praying that it will help you as well, my wonderful son.

Your boy, D

Invictus
By William Ernest Henley

Out of the night that covers me,
    Black as the pit from pole to pole,
I thank whatever gods may be
    For my unconquerable soul.

In the fell clutch of circumstance
    I have not winced nor cried aloud.
Under the bludgeonings of chance
    My head is bloody, but unbowed.

Beyond this place of wrath and tears
    Looms but the Horror of the shade,
And yet the menace of the years
    Finds and shall find me unafraid.

It matters not how strait the gate,
    How charged with punishments the scroll,
I am the master of my fate,
    I am the captain of my soul.

Jordan, NOVEMBER 5, 2010

Good to hear from you last night even though we were both a bit melancholy. As I went to bed reading about your boy, Atlas, I found my thoughts and prayers drifting to your feelings and experience of loneliness.

There may be (at least by way of my experience) nothing more difficult in life. I have wrestled with its reality at some very profound and deep levels. If you can imagine, my first conscious experience of it was a memory of standing in my crib (I don't think I was older than one and a half years old) and listening to Nana and Grandpa Moe talking and having a deep sense of being alone. I also remember when I was coming home from my best friend's house (a guy by the name of Dave Olson) where I had spent the night and saying to my Dad how, "Dave and I were going to live together forever," and him telling me that it wasn't true and someday I would grow out of this. And although his statement was true, my initial experience of this reality was feeling very alone in the world. What has become even more poignant for me is making choices like getting married, having kids, joining a church, hanging out with friends, with the hope that they would replace my loneliness with a sense of not being alone. And yet even after all these very good things I still struggle with this sense of being alone.

This has led me to rethink whether loneliness is in fact a bad thing. Could it be that loneliness is in fact an invitation, a kind of welcome mat, by which and through which we are able to encounter the deeper things of life? A guy by the name of Augustine struggled with this question and said it this way, "Our hearts are restless until they find their rest in God."[35] I am very slowly beginning to recognize this truth, which leads me to the two things I am sending you this week. The first is an article by a Catholic priest on loneliness. I like this for a number of reasons, but principally because he reflects on how loneliness was characteristic of Jesus and that the gift of loneliness is that we begin to see we need something bigger and larger than ourselves. He also ends with a wonderful poem by Hafiz who states, "Don't surrender your loneliness... let it cut deep" where we see our "need of God/Absolutely/Clear."[36] I think, if you can see it this way, your deep loneliness can be a gift to assist you in your need for God. The other is a poem called "I Am Much Too Alone in this World" by a guy whose poems I have sent you before. I love his opening line ("I am much too alone in this world, yet not alone enough to truly consecrate the hour") because it so accurately describes my own reality. Truth be told, I often feel very alone and, when people show up around me, not alone enough. That's some crazy shit right there! I also like that he places the poem in the context of a series of "wants" where he recognizes that so much of loneliness is a product of what we desire. Finally, Rilke is able to describe the hopeful note in the gift of loneliness, that it actually has the ability to make our "conscience to be true before you." I think if I had one prayer for you it would be that you sense that what this loneliness is doing in you is making you more true, complete, honest, and real. And of course these are all the things you have always desired.

As always, my deep love for you from one lonely brother to another. D

---

35 Augustine *The Works of Saint Augustine: A Translation for the 21st Century*, ed. John E. Rotelle, Boniface Ramsey, and Allan D. Fitzgerald. trans. Edmund Hill (Hyde Park, NY: New City Press, 1990).

36 "Absolutely Clear," In *The Subject Tonight Is Love: 60 Wild and Sweet Poems of Hafiz*, trans. Daniel Ladinsky (NY: Penguin Publishing Group, 2003), 50.

I Am Much Too Alone in This World, Yet Not Alone Enough
By Rainer Maria Rilke

I am much too alone in this world, yet not alone
    enough
to truly consecrate the hour.
I am much too small in this world, yet not small
    enough
to be to you just object and thing,
dark and smart.
I want my free will and want it accompanying
the path which leads to action;
and want during times that beg questions,
where something is up,
to be among those in the know,
or else be alone.

I want to mirror your image to its fullest perfection,
never be blind or too old
to uphold your weighty wavering reflection.
I want to unfold.
Nowhere I wish to stay crooked, bent;
for there I would be dishonest, untrue.
I want my conscience to be
true before you;
want to describe myself like a picture I observed

for a long time, one close up,
like a new word I learned and embraced,
like the everyday jug,
like my mother's face,
like a ship that carried me along
through the deadliest storm.

MISHPACHA REFLECTIONS
Unbent by Shame
By Lana Rocke, Friend

Joy—it's not just a gift. In a sense it is also a duty, a task to fulfill. Courage.
-Anna Kamieńska[37]

I've known Jordan since he was born. I would occasionally babysit Jordan and his brothers when they were young—an impossible task, especially when they lock you out of the house and refuse to let you in.

Like so many others, I was invited into the Hillis family system and their wild, adventurous, and wholehearted approach to life. I know Jordan endured great challenges throughout his life and I imagine they were a source of some shame. But it wasn't until my own shame was exposed to the world that I saw something else at work in Jordan.

In 2020, my dad refused to go to the hospital. He wanted to die in his own house—the house I grew up in. He got his wish. This was hard to accept as both my sister and I are nurses at the local hospital and his condition was treatable. In the days leading up to his death, my sister and I came to his home, cleaned him and his room up as best we could.

It was a holy time—a complicated grace that is forever etched into my soul—and Jordan played an important role in it.

---

37 Anna Kamieńska, *Astonishments: Selected Poems of Anna Kamieńska.* ed. Grazyna Drabik and David Curzon. trans. Grazyna Drabik and David Curzon (Brewster, MA: Paraclete Press, 2008), 116.

What follows is not the story I imagined for my father... or myself... or my kids. It's a story that is impossible to fully embrace without a community to help hold it. Perhaps then it's only fitting that Jordan and 25 of our dearest friends helped me hold what is impossible to hold.

My dad was a hardworking guy and maybe even a good man, but he was never able to shake his demons or forgive the past. His wounds festered. As a result, his life got complicated—really complicated—and debased at levels that are hard to describe. He said yes to people and things that are shocking even now.

Things began to seriously unravel seven years before he died, when he invited a young twenty-something woman named Tish to live with him. This is hard to imagine, given my dad's culturally-bound outlook on life. What's more is that Tish was a hardcore heroin addict and prostitute. Along with Tish came a host of her friends with equally complicated lives. My dad let his house become a haven for drug addicts and somehow managed to keep all of this hidden from my sister and I until the last months of his life. I don't have the words to describe how hurt, angry, shocked, and deeply ashamed I was when I found out. Of all the wounds, shame cut the deepest.

For reasons that are still unclear to me, my dad shared his house with these young women—never once coming clean with the true story of what really was going on. It was only after he died that we discovered just how involved he was in their lives. It's painful to admit to, let alone describe.

Within hours after my dad died, these young women and their

friends decided the house belonged to them. They changed the locks, set up camp, and were determined to get paid. What followed was a nightmare that included numerous calls to the police, arrests, and eventually payoffs to reclaim the property.

After a week of negotiating we came to an agreement. We would pay Tish and her friends to leave the house, but that meant getting them out while they were completely gonzo on heroin. Immediately after we escorted them out of the house and paid them off we emptied the house of all contents. To do that we needed lots of help and, given the situation, there was no way to get lots of help without also sharing the difficult story that I just outlined. Our business was out there. No way to hide it.

More than 25 friends and family showed up on short notice to help us vacate the house. They emptied all its contents and did so in a way that I will never forget—firmly, graciously upholding the dignity of my father, my sister and I, and even Tish and her friends. This is the house my sister and I grew up in. We occupied the bedroom where Tish slept, did drugs, and turned tricks with countless men. We even found out later from police reports and transactional records that my father kept in a notebook that a guy died in that room from an overdose. This is what our community held in trust and care.

That Saturday was surreal. Our friends carefully picked up hundreds of used needles off the floor of my old bedroom and loaded three large dumpsters to take to the landfill. One friend helped sort papers, another tried in vain to find some small treasure in my dad's locked desk, desperately wanting to find something redeemable for my sake. Everyone pitched in with love and even good humor and this included my own sons and their friends.

And that's when it happened. That's when I saw a glimpse of heaven on earth.

Jordan not only entered into my shame and the shame of my family that day, he walked into it without hesitation. He cared for it and covered it with a kind of dignity and honor that I did not think possible, and he did this without a word. He dove into the task with a singularity of purpose and laser-like focus that was noticed by all who gathered that day. He picked up used needles, ripped up blood stained carpet, tossed out unmentionable paraphernalia that I wish I could forget and I wish 25 of our closest friends could unsee. Jordan did this with an intensity born of someone who knows the burn of shame. He also did it with a holy disregard for the degradation before him. He insisted on holding my father's dignity and the value of my childhood home and all who occupied it. He did all of this as one who knows what it means to have their shame held with immense grace and dignity. Jordan became the icon of that experience.

At some point that day we paused to share a simple meal—pizza. We gathered in my childhood living room and prayed for my father, our family, the house, and the complicated relationships he left behind.

My husband, Kris, thanked the people who gathered. He acknowledged the painful reality of the situation. With colorful language and a warm smile, he admitted to the group that my father was "a mother fucker," but much more than that. He said my father was created in God's image—that he is a child of God and thanked the group for holding the dignity of my dad. He acknowledged that Tish was a drug addict and prostitute. But he also said that she too is a child of God created in God's image and thanked the community for holding her dignity. And then, in a quiet voice, he thanked the community for holding the dignity of my sister and I in our own brokenness and shame—they prayed for us.

Between dump runs, used hypodermic needles and cold pizza in my childhood living room, I saw a glimpse of heaven on earth. Jordan was there, in the center of it all, standing tall. He refused to be bent by the shame before us. Jordan helped me hold my father's life—his complicated and messed up life and the lives of those he opened himself up to, not in contempt, but in love. It's because of this that I am not a complete wreck.

Jordan was not scandalized by what seemed so scandalous to me. Jordan was motivated by something that allowed him to embrace and hold my shame (and maybe his too) with such dignity and honor. From where I sit, the thing at work in Jordan that day was joy—not the bubbly kind of joy of pop culture—but the deeper kind of joy that calls forth a highly concentrated kind of sobriety and clarity of purpose that makes the unendurable endurable. I will always love Jordan for giving me that gift.

Jordan,

I hope this letter finds you well. I was just looking at the file on
my computer where I save my letters to you. This is number
31. Assuming you are in until July 3rd (which I think if I
remember is your targeted date) I have 29 more letters to write
to you before you are home. That is a delightful thought…you
and I are more than halfway to the Promised Land!

Well, you have redeemed yourself through *The Sicilian* after
that shit-storm of a book you gave me in *Atlas*. Two pages into
it I could immediately understand why you like the book so
much. The characters are compelling, it beautifully describes
the landscape of Sicily, and the plot is captivating. I have been
in bed as early as 8:00 p.m. so as to continue reading the book.
So don't worry, your literary reputation is still intact!

I enjoyed talking with you last night. It was very encouraging
to hear the energy in your voice, the routine you have been able
to get back into, and the hope I sensed in your outlook. There
are very few things that give me more energy than sensing that
you and your brothers are doing well.

To that end the poem I am sending you this week captures a bit
of that sense of encouragement that I felt in my conversation
with you. It is another one by Mary (oh, how I do love my girl!)
called "Invitation." In some ways it is a very simple poem, at
least in the way it is framed. In essence she is describing the life
of goldfinches as they go about their day—they have "gathered
in a field of thistles for a musical battle" and they "drink the air"
and other related things that any normal goldfinch would be

about. But upon closer examination she uses the goldfinch as a model for those simple things in life and how we should live our life. I think this is best articulated (which I also find deeply convicting and illuminating) when she writes, "they strive melodiously... not for the sake of winning, but for sheer delight and gratitude... just to be alive." In reading this I become instantly aware of how often so much of who I am is about the "sake of winning"—making money, being successful, looking okay, etc. The challenge, she then poses to us, is whether we develop the discipline to "not walk by... attend to this rather ridiculous performance," that it might result in a decision to "change your life."

I don't know where you might find a "goldfinch" this week to think about—maybe a celly, a good book, your feeling after your workout, but take the time to allow the sheer beauty of it to "change your life."

Your boy, D

Invitation
By Mary Oliver

Oh do you have time
    to linger
        for just a little while
            out of your busy

and very important day
    for the goldfinches
        that have gathered
            in a field of thistles

for a musical battle,
    to see who can sing
        the highest note,
            or the lowest,

or the most expressive of mirth,
    or the most tender?
        Their strong, blunt beaks
            drink the air

as they strive
    melodiously
        not for your sake
            and not for mine

and not for the sake of winning
    but for sheer delight and gratitude—
        believe us, they say,
            it is a serious thing

just to be alive
    on this fresh morning
        in the broken world.
            I beg of you,

do not walk by
    without pausing
        to attend to this
            rather ridiculous performance.

It could mean something.
It could mean everything.
It could be what Rilke meant, when he wrote:
You must change your life.

Jordan,   NOVEMBER 19, 2010

It was good talking to you last night. Upon listening to you describe your neck I immediately prayed for your healing. Any progress? I will also pray a prayer for you at Mass tonight and light a votive candle—the full meal deal for you, my brother.

In waking up this morning and grabbing the paper, I encountered the headline "McNeil Island to close." Although we talked about it last night, I was surprised to see it displayed so boldly in the paper this morning. It must be kind of wild out there right now. How does the atmosphere feel? Are things more relaxed or more tense? Do the guards give you more freedom or less? It is kind of wild, maybe even symbolic, to think you will be a part of the last group to occupy a place that has been around so long. It is also my hope that with all that is taking place around McNeil, such as the replacing of the guards, transferring of the inmates, etc., that perhaps you will be given a break and get out earlier than anticipated. Wouldn't that be nice!

I am loving your book recommendation regarding *The Sicilian*. Along with it being very well written, it is also a riveting plot. I will tell you that I am afraid that things are not going to end well for our boy.

This week I am sending you a poem that, in effect, is a prayer. I should add that this is one of the things I have always loved about poems, their ability to behave as prayers. As a consequence, I have prayed poems for different people. It helps me find words for people that I often don't feel I have myself. This prayer/poem is by Thomas Merton who was a monk. I think I have told you about him before. One of the things that I deeply appreciate about Merton (and I think you will too) is his absolute commitment to tell the truth about himself and the world regardless of how uncomfortable that makes him feel. He says that the ultimate inspiration of prayer is "our own nothingness." This makes great sense to me when I consider who I am and what I am not. He goes on to say that the trajectory of prayer moves towards—and I love this idea—mercy. More than any single thing I have discovered in my years of walking with Jesus is the incomparable power of mercy. Jo, it is always about mercy. Never, ever forget that. And then finally he ends with the idea that it should move us to asking God for things because the person who does not ask does not know "his own need for God." Perfect ending.

Alright my brother, always good to write to you.

Your boy, D

Prayer[38]
By Thomas Merton
From *No Man is an Island*

"Prayer is inspired by God in the depth of our own nothingness. It is the movement of trust, of gratitude, of adoration, or of sorrow that places us before God, seeing both Him and ourselves in the light of His infinite truth, and moves us to ask Him for the mercy, the spiritual strength, the material help that we all need. The one whose prayer is so pure that he never asks God for anything does not know who God is, and does not know who he is himself: for he does not know his own need of God."

---

38 Thomas Merton, *No Man Is an Island* (Boston: Shambhala, 2005), 44.

Jordan,   NOVEMBER 25, 2010

Greetings my brother! It was good to hear your voice last night.
I am sorry I couldn't talk longer, but Mark, Mike, and I were
right in the middle of one of the famous Hillis competitions.
Mark was reading from a list of books on his computer and
Mike and I were "hitting the buzzer" to see who could guess
the author of the book first. Sadly, Mike got the better of me. I
suppose this is the underside of being surrounded by talented
siblings. You know a little bit about that.

I just finished *The Sicilian* and you have redeemed yourself. It
was a very good book, although I should say I finished it with
my worst fear confirmed—Turi's death. What I did not expect
was his right-hand-man's betrayal. Not that anything should
surprise one regarding that world, but it was sad nonetheless.
What was particularly intriguing to me was how close the
story of Turi and his colleagues followed the life of Christ. I
don't know how much you have either read or heard, but the
story of Christ (which of course is what makes it such a great
story) is about a man who is born a king, but decides to never
exercise this authority in the way he was entitled. He comes to
a land that is being ruled by Rome and a puppet government
led by Herod, decides to pull together a "gang" (called the
disciples) of everyday people, takes the side of the poor and
marginalized, and ends up dying the worst imaginable death
(on a cross) as a result of being betrayed by one of his closest
associates (Judas). You see the similarities, do you not? How
closely Turi's life is patterned after Jesus. Of course the huge
difference is that even death can't defeat Jesus, unlike Turi. All
that to say, thanks for recommending the book in that it was

both a great read and you got your reputation back for being literate. We will talk before you receive this letter, but what would you recommend next?

This book got me thinking about the poem I would send you. This one is called "The Coming" by R.S. Thomas where he wonderfully describes the decision that God, in the person of Christ, made to come to our world. One of the things that I like about this poem is the way the world, in all of its "scorched land... crusted buildings... a bright Serpent... with slime," is always being held in "his hand." I don't know about you, but those are often the very things that people use to say there is no God. The truth of course (and this is a great mystery) is that no matter how bad things are (and they can get awfully bad at times, as you well know) we are never not being held by God. Do you believe this to be true? I often think that this simple truth may be the thing that separates those who are Holy and those who are not. That it is not about our lifestyle—the moral or immoral things we have done—but whether we believe, regardless of what we experience, that God holds the world and us in his hand.

The poem moves into the second stanza and unveils what this God through the Son decides to do. I love the description of the world ("as though waiting for a vanished April") because it reminds me of those wonderfully lovely spring days in the Northwest. Do you remember those kinds of things? When you first sense the sun is becoming warm, when you can smell the freshly mown grass, when you can think about that first barbecue? I like to think of the world in this way. But then the clincher: The Son who has infinite choices before him chooses to come to us when he says, "Let me go there." What is particularly important for me is the idea that God, in Jesus, actually chooses us over and against being forced to come to us.

I deeply hope and pray that you will be warmed by the simple elegance of that truth, Jo: Jesus chose and continues to choose you all the time.

Your very grateful father for you, D

The Coming[39]
By R.S. Thomas

And God held in his hand
A small globe. Look, he said.
The son looked. Far off,
As through water, he saw
a scorched land of fierce
colour. The light burned
There: crusted buildings
Cast their shadows; a bright
Serpent, a river
Uncoiled itself, radiant
With slime.

On a bare
Hill a bare tree saddened
The sky. Many people
Held out their thin arms
To it, as though waiting
For a vanished April
To return to its crossed
Boughs. The son watched
Them. Let me go there, he said.

---

39 Ronald S. Thomas, 2002. *R.S. Thomas: Everyman Poetry*, ed. Anthony Thwaite (London: Orion House, 1996), 72.

MISHPACHA REFLECTIONS
Norway
By Mike Hillis, Uncle

Like any family, ours is made up of a series of stories that vacillate between the apocryphal and the authentic, those that we wish were true and those that are. One of the authentic stories that surfaced earlier and often and that later shaped a second authentic story I experienced with Jordan was around *To Kill A Mockingbird.*

Early in Jordan's life, when he was roughly five, Ryan was seven, and Patrick was nine, my brother Dave posted on their refrigerator a list from the Tacoma Public Library of 100 must-read books. The way the story goes, Dave told his boys that either he would read these books to them, they would read them themselves, or they would watch a film version (so long as it was an accurate representation of the book). This rather lighthearted plan ended up unveiling a remarkable truth about Jordan.

At about 10 books into the experience Dave was reading *To Kill A Mockingbird.* As Dave began to hear that sound that all parents long for at night—the slow, labored breathing of sleeping children—he closed the book and began to head out of the bedroom when he heard Jordan's voice (already sounding like a sonorous alto sax) say, "I know who the mockingbird is, D." Dave responded, "Jordan, most likely not. There are doctoral theses written about who the mockingbird is and we are only in the third chapter." Jordan persisted, "It is Boo Radley." And with that Dave said goodnight, having already been made aware from teachers' reports that he had a son who was going to have a very hard time in school, but in this one singular moment Jordan showed his particular insight.

Nearly a decade passed when on a cold, February morning in 2001 we welcomed Jordan to join us in Oslo, Norway during a year of scholarship and study for my family.

To say Jo had been struggling with school would be an understatement, as Jordan's teachers and his family had foreseen. Each year we would hear reports of Jordan getting through another year by the skin of his teeth. We all knew he was intelligent and insightful, but the education system as it was structured was not only unhelpful for Jordan, on its ugliest days it perpetrated a kind of violence that had him feeling worthless, demoralized, and stupid. It was in this context that his parents felt that drastic measures were needed for an academic reset. The plan was for him to live with us for a minimum of a couple months and, through a more customized "homeschool" plan, hopefully Jordan could renew his confidence by becoming familiar with his latent brilliance.

When he first arrived he was in bad shape. Like anybody who has been immersed in a system that under-appreciates and under-values them, he had little to no confidence left. It was in this context that I sat him down and said, "Ok Jo, here's what I would like to do. It's really dark and cold here for about 20 hours a day during the winter, so I'm going to ask you to read every day."

"Read what?" he asked warily.

I replied, "It doesn't really matter; I just want you to read something that captures your imagination and will keep your mind engaged for the next couple of months. What are you interested in?"

"Organized crime," he said.

Not the response I was expecting, but also not surprising. Jordan was eclectic. He was already beginning to emerge as a poet, he loved to rap, and he enjoyed all genres of good storytelling since he was a young child. "Ok... yeah, that should work. Let's jump on the tram tomorrow, head into the city, and buy some books. I'm sure they will have some stuff you're interested in."

We did just that and ended up finding a number of books about the Irish mob and the Italian mafia. I thought we were set for the long winter in front of us, knowing that we'd honored Jo's choices, but, as it turned out, we were just getting started.

When we got back to our home, I told him that he could start with whatever book he wanted and that the plan would be for us to talk about what he was reading over the course of the next couple of months.

Jo looked down and was quiet for a moment before he said, "Ummm, I'm not sure I can do this. I've never really read a full book by myself."

I still feel the ache in me upon hearing that response. Here was an exceptionally bright young man who was hobbled, harmed, and hurt as he reflected out loud with me. As an educator, I knew the depth of difficulty that awaited him if this current reality remained. So I carefully ventured, "But you can read, right?"

"Yeah, I know how to read… I just don't read."

"Ok, so that's what we will work on. Does that work?"

"Yeah, but I probably need some help." And it was in that short response that the young man who knew who the mockingbird was emerged: a frail but fortified young man that wanted to give it a try.

"Cool—so let's do this: You read a chapter, I'll read the same chapter, and we'll talk about it as we work our way through each book. Sound good?"

"Yep," and off he went to read the first chapter of a book on the Irish mob. I remember thinking at the time that I wasn't sure what would come of this, but if we did make some progress and Jordan took to the material and the experience of reading, it may change the trajectory of his education and how he sees himself as a student going forward.

The next day, he said, "Ok, I'm ready." The eagerness in his voice surprised me in a delightful way. Having spent time with a number of people who have struggled to read, that first meeting can be like scaling Mount Everest. People are often defeated and even deadened by one more reminder of why they weren't reading in the first place. So I quickly scanned the chapter to make sure that I knew what we would be talking about to be as good a partner as I could be for him.

The result? Over the course of the next 30 minutes, Jo was able to recall the entire chapter verbatim, picking up things that I barely retained or even knew existed in the first place. I looked at him with a mixture of unbridled pride combined with an unalloyed shock; a grateful clarity with a deep puzzlement. All I could utter was, "You don't need me for this Jo. Do your thing."

And he did. Over the next two months Jo finished all six of the books we had originally purchased, bought a few more on a follow up trip to the bookstore, and, most importantly, became an accomplished reader despite a significant learning disability.

This love for story never ceased for Jo and I can recall having soulful conversations with him through the years about *The Grapes of Wrath* (the hardships confronting family and the resilience to survive), *Crime and Punishment* (the hubris of Raskolnikov and his movement to redemption), and *Just Revenge* (the impact of losing one's family and the compulsion for revenge). That little boy who knew who the mockingbird was surfaced and resurfaced time and again and became someone that the Hillis family relied on to tell our stories.

WINTER

Jordan,   DECEMBER 3, 2010

Well, here I am again writing the first letter of December and
one of the last of 2010. My sense is that you and I are both
ready to put 2010 behind us! What a shit-storm of a year.

I need to first apologize for the lateness of this letter. My
computer jammed up on Friday so I am actually writing this
on Monday. Such is the result of living in a world that often
depends on things that are outside of our control.

I enjoyed our time last Sunday. Conversations with you are, of
course, always enjoyable, but it was particularly nice to watch
you and Ryan interact. There are very few things in life that are
more pleasing to me than witnessing the good friendships that
the three of you have. When all is said and done, it will be the
quality of relationships that we have that will stand out as most
important and lasting. I think this is one of the reasons why,
when asked by a young lawyer, "What must I do to inherit
eternal life?" Jesus responded by saying, "Love God with all
of your heart, soul, and mind; and your neighbor as yourself."
It appears that Jesus deeply understood this same truth about
the importance and power of relationships. The young lawyer
didn't like the answer and so proceeded to ask Jesus, "Who
is my neighbor?", hoping to justify himself. Jesus responded
with one of the great stories (called the Good Samaritan)
where he described a guy who ended up loving someone who
represented all that was despised by society. In effect, he was
saying everyone is your neighbor.[40] All that to say, one of the

---

40 Summarization of Luke 10:25-37

things I greatly admire about you is the way you have loved people, whoever they might be; whatever shape or size they might come in; regardless of what they may have done. It is very much the Spirit of Jesus in you and for that I am better because of you.

This week I am sending you a poem by Chuang Tzu called "The Need to Win." The reason I am sending it is it ties into what I said in the previous paragraph. If relationships are the most important thing then the immediate question is why do we not make them more of a priority? I think Tzu is on to something when he suggests that it is because we think we must win. As he states so eloquently, "But the prize divides him. He cares. He thinks more about winning than of shooting." I often think about this as it relates to relationships, how often, when we meet with someone, we think more of trying to prove our point than finding out what that person thinks. And ultimately, as Tzu suggests, this perspective literally "drains him (us) of power." Pretty deep, huh?

I trust you will have a great week.

Your boy, D

The Need to Win
By Chuang Tzu

When an archer is shooting for nothing,
He has all his skill.
If he shoots for a brass buckle,
He is already nervous.
If he shoots for a prize of gold,
He goes blind
Or sees two targets—
He is out of his mind!

His skill has not changed. But the prize
Divides him. He cares.
He thinks more of winning
Than of shooting—
And the need to win
Drains him of power.

Jordan,   DECEMBER 10, 2010

Greetings on this high, holy day: namely P-Did's 29th birthday! Can you believe it? That boy is quickly approaching his fourth decade of life. He has lived enough life (as you and Ryan have as well) to be pushing 50.

I have good news—I just finished an email correspondence with a friend, who, as I write, is sending a letter to Mr. Hubert to notify him that his company is officially willing to hire you in the warehouse. Moreover, he indicates in his letter that he is thinking long-term, where he imagines positions you can grow into, if you would like to stay around. How about that? Although I know you are already aware of this, make sure you give a special prayer of thanks and, when you see him, hug your Uncle Mark. While I had a bit to do with this whole process, it was Mark who did the heavy lifting and delivered the goods. You have got some people who are seriously committed to your ass! I have enclosed the letter.

The poem I am sending you this week, in light of the conversations we have had about your sleeping and nightmares, is a poem called "Last Night As I Was Sleeping," by Antonio Machado. I first ran across this poem about five years ago at a poetry reading and instantly fell in love with it for a number of reasons. One of the primary reasons is how important the reality of sleep is for all of us. It is one of those things (don't you think?) that we all take for granted until we have a bad night of sleep and then we go crazy. I know you experienced a bit of that working graveyard. He goes on to talk about four dreams that are "marvelous errors." This phrase strikes me in part by the juxtaposition, where the thing is "marvelous" but that it also is viewed as an "error." This has often been my experience, where I have good things happen not *because of* but *in spite of* what I had hoped. Do you agree? My primary purpose for sending you this poem, though, is in the second stanza where he writes, "And the golden bees were making white combs and sweet honey from my old failures." This is my prayer for you Jo: You will actually experience in your dreams the transformation of some of your failures that have kept you up, and even haunted you a bit, into sweet honey.

I will continue to pray this poem for you in the days and nights ahead.

Your boy,

D

Last Night As I Was Sleeping
By Antonio Machado

Last night as I was sleeping,
I dreamt—marvelous error!—
that a spring was breaking

out in my heart.
I said: Along which secret aqueduct,
Oh water, are you coming to me,
water of a new life
that I have never drunk?

Last night as I was sleeping,
I dreamt—marvelous error!—
that I had a beehive
here inside my heart.
And the golden bees
were making white combs
and sweet honey
from my old failures.

Last night as I was sleeping,
I dreamt—marvelous error!—
that a fiery sun was giving
light inside my heart.
It was fiery because I felt

warmth as from a hearth,
and sun because it gave light
and brought tears to my eyes.

Last night as I slept,
I dreamt—marvelous error!—
that it was God I had
here inside my heart.

Jordan,   DECEMBER 17, 2010

As I am sure you are experiencing, it is a beautiful day in the Northwest. It is the kind of day that makes all of us who have grown up here treasure it so as to live through the countless days of gray skies and relentless rain. Now that I think of it, you are probably (other than a bit of barbed wire, bad food, and iron bars) in an even better position to enjoy this day by way of your beachside proximity!

It was good to talk with you last night. I was very impressed with the maturity you projected in light of all the moving parts—inmates fighting, friends being moved, your future placement up in the air, etc.—that could easily throw someone less mature into a dark and hopeless place. I hope you sense this growth in yourself.

I did send an email this morning to a good friend making a request that his firm hire you for the next six months until your "official time" is over and you can go and work in the warehouse. Of course, by the time you get this letter I will probably have some definitive news for you. As I know you will, let's pray this will be a positive outcome.

JD's tournament starts tomorrow. Can you believe that it is the 7th annual? The opening ceremony is tomorrow at 3:00 p.m. so I am going to show up (given that Leadership Foundations is one of the sponsors), hear Mark make a little speech (you know how he loves to do that!), and watch a bit of the game. It has been a long-ass time since I have sat in the bleachers at Al Davies. I will never forget the many times I sat there watching you hoist up those deep threes that you were so famous for. It still makes me chuckle to think about it.

In honor of JD's tourney I am sending you the poem that Mike and I wrote for his obituary and that now hangs on the wall at Al Davies. I don't know if you know the story, but Mike and I wrote the poem in about 30 minutes at the old G Street home. It was one of those moments where you don't even feel like you are writing and creating anything as much as recording and listening to what has already been written. Does that make sense and have you had that experience? Anyway there are two things I like most about this poem. The first, of course, is the image of the jump shot and using it to hint at those transcendent truths that we all long for. My working premise is anything done well—a football pass, writing, eating, work, etc.—hints at the beauty of life. The second thing I like about this poem is that last sentence which has, in my mind, layers of meaning: "A jump shot framed, For Evermore." That's some good shit right there, Jo!

I will see you on Sunday with your boy, Mr. O.

Affectionately, D

JD Hillis Memoriam Poem
By Dave and Mike Hillis

The sound of the ball,
The slide of the feet,
The feint of the head,
The gathering underneath,
Rising upon the balls of his feet,
Ball poised upon fingertips,
A jump shot framed,
For Evermore.

MISHPACHA REFLECTIONS
Attaboy
By Todd Silver, Friend

I remember when Dave brought the wee lads—Patrick, Ryan, and Jordan—to our house once to help unload a truck full of firewood into our basement. They were tiny and could barely carry one log but did so with vigor and much laughter.

In the years that followed I've had the honor of being Jordan's friend, employer, and rowing coach. He always displayed a warm, welcoming, and adventurous spirit that I've deeply enjoyed. As an employee, Jo set the all-time record for peer "attaboy" recognitions in our firm. We had a system where fellow employees could write a note of recognition, appreciation, and encouragement to their colleagues to be shared at month's end. Jo received five in one month! We'd read these cards out loud to the crew and you could just see him glow as each one was shared and many congratulatory hugs ensued. His coworkers came to love and appreciate him deeply.

A few years later Jordan approached me about learning to row a single rowing shell. This skinny watercraft is extremely tippy and a challenge to master, especially on the Puget Sound's choppy open waters. On his first day out, Jordan capsized his boat three times! Each time his head bobbed out with a giant smile and then, righting his craft, he'd continue on with buoyant enthusiasm. One of the couples at our rowing club even pulled me aside to comment on his warmth and respectful nature—big smile, warm handshake, "Yes sir, no ma'am," and always asking for tips on how to improve his stroke. That was Jo.

It wasn't long until he'd mastered the rowing shell and was showing promise as he plied the waters of the Puget Sound. When we rowed together we sometimes found ourselves in the waters offshore of Dave and Teresa's front window. I'm sure their hearts were full as they watched him stream across the bay. After only three months of training, he entered the Commencement Bay Regatta, a challenging six-mile, triangular, open-water course. This race starts in an "Oklahoma Stampede style" mass start with competitors of all kinds, side by side, pulling and paddling their hearts out toward the first-turn buoy two miles in the distance. As the field spread out I could tell that many of the experienced racers were wondering who the heck was this guy in that sleek gray racing shell? A ringer from the East Coast perhaps? Jo worked his way through the traffic and crossed the finish line taking second place in his boat class. Amazing! He was so proud to get his award as the crowd cheered for this rookie from Tacoma. Fortunately for them, Jordan's work in Alaska kept him away from future competitions, but I'm sure he'd have become one of the Northwest's premier open water racers—if he'd had the chance to stay in the game.

Dear Jordan, DECEMBER 24, 2010

My letter is coming to you the "day before Christmas" which you will remember is a bit of a rendition on the famous poem titled "The Night before Christmas." Whether day or night, I find this particular Christmas to be bittersweet. Of course the bitter part of it is that you are not with us. The sweet part is the knowledge of how well you have navigated these past few months and, most importantly, that you, in your own unique way, have said 'yes' to the reason that makes Christmas real: the person of Jesus.

This sweet part of Christmas came to me while I was reading this morning, praying a little bit, and reflecting on "all things Hillis." I came across this verse that made me think of you. The Apostle Paul (who wrote much of the New Testament) is ruminating on the idea of Christmas, God becoming incarnate in the person of Jesus. I should add that while the word "incarnate" sounds a bit big it actually means "in the state of meat" or, said another way, something that we can taste, feel, and see. As a result, Christmas literally means that God came in the form of meat so we can digest him. Pretty wild! Anyway, Paul is attempting to try and prove how people like you and I can know that this is true. His answer is that the Holy Spirit has set up camp in our hearts and that the way we know this to be true is that we are now able to say something that we could not previously state: "Abba, Father." This phrase is very powerful because it is in Aramaic (this was Jesus' first language) and the word literally means "daddy." Stated another way, now for the first time, and as a result of saying yes to Jesus, we can have an intimate relationship with God. So much so that we can call him a "daddy," where we no longer have to be scared, worried, wondering if we are going to be punished, but rather we can sit on God's lap.[41] The reason I go off on this theological ramble is that I want you to know (and I should add that it is very obvious in your life) that when you made the decision you, in effect, have God as a "daddy." Moreover, any time you doubt or wonder if you actually have this relationship, you can remind yourself that your ability to cry out to God as "Abba, Father" is a confirmation that this truth is very alive in you. This is a very long way of saying why Christmas, along with the bitter, is also sweet to me this year: This truth has happened to you.

As a result of all of this, you would think I would send you a Christmas poem—something that has a bit of Santa, reindeers, and elves on the secular side or, manger, wise men, Mary, and Joseph on the religious side. Instead, what I am sending you is one of Shakespeare's sonnets (#116). Along with all the plays he wrote, he also scribed some remarkable sonnets. This one has always appealed to me because it so reflects what I think something like Christmas is about. In effect, he describes the nature of love. Whatever else Christmas is, it is about love. His line "Love is not love which alters when it alteration finds: O no! it is an ever-fixed mark… and is never shaken" describes the essence of the Christ. God loves us not to change or "alter" us, but to allow us to become who we were meant to become. This is my own way of saying that I am so happy and thankful that you are you! That my love for you is not to change you or make you something different, but to celebrate and cheer on who you are. This, my young brother, is why I am able to celebrate this Christmas.

I love you more than you can possibly know. D

---

41 Summarization of Galatians 4

Sonnet 116
By William Shakespeare

Let me not to the marriage of true minds
Admit impediments. Love is not love
Which alters when it alteration finds,
Or bends with the remover to remove:
O no! it is an ever-fixed mark
That looks on tempests and is never shaken;
It is the star to every wandering bark,
Whose worth's unknown, although his height be taken.
Love's not Time's fool, though rosy lips and cheeks
Within his bending sickle's compass come:
Love alters not with his brief hours and weeks,
But bears it out even to the edge of doom.
    If this be error and upon me proved,
    I never writ, nor no man ever loved.

Jordan,

Greetings my brother on this last day of 2010! The next letter I send you will have a 2011 date attached to it. It is amazing, is it not, how time continues to march on? I should also add that hearing about the confirmation of your work release opportunity was a great Christmas present and New Years Day wish. To think about you being nearby, accessible, able to hang out with the family, eat some of the food that you must be jonesing for big time—it will be a great homecoming.

I don't know if you heard, but your boy P-Did is in Morocco. He and Teresa decided to get a little R&R in an Arabic-speaking country. I am trying to remember in your travels how close you got to getting there? I know it's just across the water from the tip of Spain. Either way, you know your boy is going to be living some life.

I was reading about Meyer Lansky last night and saw for the first time some of his "darkness" in his relationship with his first wife and their kids. Up and till this point he has seemed, similar to Carlo Gambino, like an "honest gangster" where they were good business people, eschewed violence, and cared for their friends. In reading about Meyer's relationship with his wife, however, I am reconsidering my opinion. That boy was a dog to her. It is really quite tragic and made me think a bit about my own relationship to your mom. I am also curious as to what you and your brothers sense about our relationship. Has it been something you have admired, struggled with, wondered about, etc.? At some point I would love to get your reflections.

I am sending you a poem this week that is a bit of a reflection on what the New Year may hold for you and I going forward. It is from Mary and it is called "The Summer Day." Now it may seem odd to send you a summer poem in mid-winter, but I think the poem is reflective of what the new year can mean. I think the fact that the poem starts out with three questions is quite good in that any new start, at least in my way of thinking, begins with a good question. I also like the fact that in the middle of the poem she states that "I don't know exactly what a prayer is," although you get the sense that "falling in the grass" being "idle in the fields" etc. is a part of her answer. Ultimately prayer is being aware, which I think you do a very good job of. But the most important line and the one that makes me think about you here at the end of 2010 and beginning in 2011 is the last line: "Tell me, what is it you plan to do with your one wild and precious life?" Isn't that a great line and doesn't it, in many ways, say it all? I am very, very, excited to see how you will answer this question in moving forward with the "wild and precious life" that you are.

Much love, D

The Summer Day
By Mary Oliver

Who made the world?
Who made the swan, and the black bear?
Who made the grasshopper?
This grasshopper, I mean—
the one who has flung herself out of the grass,
the one who is eating sugar out of my hand,
who is moving her jaws back and forth instead of up and down—
who is gazing around with her enormous and complicated eyes.
Now she lifts her pale forearms and thoroughly washes her face.
Now she snaps her wings open, and floats away.
I don't know exactly what a prayer is.
I do know how to pay attention, how to fall down
into the grass, how to kneel down in the grass,
how to be idle and blessed, how to stroll through the fields,
which is what I have been doing all day.
Tell me, what else should I have done?
Doesn't everything die at last, and too soon?
Tell me, what is it you plan to do
with your one wild and precious life?

Jordan,   JANUARY 7, 2011

Another Friday... it is hard to believe how many of these letters
we now have behind us. Moreover, the idea that this will be my
second to last letter to you at McNeil feels even more surreal.
Whatever else I know about life, Jo, it is this: Change is always
at play. And it is in light of this reality of change and how it is
honestly engaged and applied that becomes one of the strongest
characteristics of a person who can truly call themselves mature.
The reason I reflect on this is to encourage you. You have had
a wild ride this past year regarding change. Just to name a
few—arrested, convicted, placed; in County, Shelton, McNeil;
no job, shit job, current job; different cellies and colleagues
including Jemel, Zach, Kris, Old Blue, and the crazy guy in
the tank; time alone, time with many, time at night, time in
the day; and through it all you have grown, learned, adapted,
and decided. I am very proud of the way you have negotiated
this and it has given me courage to face the changes in my life
as well. Thanks.

This idea—change and how we respond to it—leads me to the
poem I am sending you this week. I think if you read into my
first paragraph that the key is for us to grab the proverbial bull
by the horns and take control, or if life gives you lemons you
make lemonade, I would be leading you astray. I am convinced
that being able to make do of the change that comes at us
is precisely to the degree that we don't take control but (as
one theologian put it) "relax into the struggle."[42] To that end,

---

42 James Alison, *Jesus the Forgiving Victim: Listening for the Unheard Voice* (Glenville, IL: Doers Publishing, 2013).

this poem, "Love is the Funeral Pyre," describes what I think is the ultimate act of faithfulness: laying our body (intellect, emotions, and physical) in the hands of God who will take better care of us than we ever could ourselves. In this poem God as love is the "funeral pyre" where the poet writes he lays his "living body." That body, made up of (and I love this line) "false notions of myself that once caused fear, pain," has now turned to ash. I sometimes think because we are so fearful of turning into "ash" we would rather hold onto our "false notions." But the poem goes on to say that if we do let go of our self there will be a rising "through the eyes of angels" and will actually be characterized by "screams from the guts of infinite existence itself." Then rightly the poem concludes where it begins: "love is the funeral pyre."

My sense is you have done this very thing with all the change that has come at you. While you could have easily run away from or become hardened to it, you instead have laid your body on the "funeral pyre." The result is a remarkable transformation in you that makes me tremble when I think about it.

Thanks for doing this very brave thing, Jo.

Your boy, D

Love Is The Funeral Pyre
By Hafiz
Translation by Daniel Ladinsky

Love is
The funeral pyre
Where I have laid my living body.

All the false notions of myself
That once caused fear, pain,

Have turned to ash
As I neared God.

What has risen
From the tangled web of thought and sinew

Now shines with jubilation
Through the eyes of angels

And screams from the guts of
Infinite existence
Itself.

Love is the funeral pyre
Where the heart must lay
Its body.

Jordan,   JANUARY 14, 2011

I always wondered what it would feel like to write this letter to you in McNeil. To think, starting next week, that I will send my future letters to you at a different address, knowing that it goes to a place that is in the city, and that it will be read by you not in a cell but a room—well, in truth, it actually makes me both happy and sad.

I am happy because I know what it means for you to get out of McNeil. It has been six long months full of very dark times, bad bosses, not enough food that's (when you do get it) shitty at best. I also think of how hard—particularly the time Whit and I came out to see you on Ryan and Kasi's wedding day— some of the visits were with you knowing that we were going back to home as you returned to the cell.

And maybe sad isn't quite the word, but I am feeling "something" regarding your leaving that place. Maybe it's gratefulness or thankfulness… I am not completely sure. Somewhere though I do find that I have a deep appreciation for what has happened to me over these past six months and what I sense has happened in you. As for me, your time at McNeil has taught me how to persevere, love in the midst of not being able to do anything practically, pray for you knowing that only God will know the content of my prayer, and ultimately teach me to be grateful in all things. So if my being a bit sad that this is my last letter to you at this address seems a bit strange, I think it is because McNeil helped me grow.

In light of this being the last letter at McNeil, I thought the poem I am sending you should reflect this reality. To that end I am sending you a poem by—can I say it?—our favorite, Mary. This one is called "Heavy." The reason I send it is because, at least from my estimation, she so accurately describes my own pilgrimage with you at McNeil (and maybe yours?) with a transparent reflection on both the pain and the joy of it all. I love the way it begins with "That time I thought I could not go any closer to grief without dying" which so captures my initial feelings on you being arrested, convicted, and sent away. Immediately though—and this too was my experience—she goes on to write "I went closer and I did not die. Surely God had his hand in this." I am learning this truth very slowly. I find myself so very afraid about many things, and yet as I go closer I do not die. But the most important part of the poem for me—principally because it reminds me of a deep truth and it gives me words for what I have so admired in you is this: "Then said my friend Daniel, (brave even among lions), 'It's not the weight you carry but how you carry it—books, bricks, grief— it's all in the way you embrace it, balance it, carry it when you cannot, and would not put it down.' So I went on practicing." I cannot stress enough to you how I have so deeply honored the way you have carried the "books, bricks, grief" of your time at McNeil. As a result you have been shaping (whether you know it or not) the way I carry the "books, bricks, grief" of my life.

So how does this time at McNeil end? Maybe it's upon leaving your cell for the last time you simply thank God for it all.

Your very hopeful and grateful father, D

Heavy
By Mary Oliver

That time
I thought I could not
go any closer to grief
without dying

I went closer,
and I did not die.
Surely God
had his hand in this,

as well as friends.
Still, I was bent,
and my laughter,
as the poet said,

was nowhere to be found.
Then said my friend Daniel,
(brave even among lions),
"It's not the weight you carry

but how you carry it—
books, bricks, grief—
it's all in the way
you embrace it, balance it, carry it

when you cannot, and would not,
put it down."
So I went practicing.
Have you noticed?

Have you heard
the laughter
that comes, now and again,
out of my startled mouth?

How I linger
to admire, admire, admire
the things of this world
that are kind, and maybe

also troubled—
roses in the wind,
the sea geese on the steep waves,
a love
to which there is no reply?

MISHPACHA REFLECTIONS
Freedom
By Ryan Hillis, Brother

The day finally arrived when, instead of *me* taking the ferry to McNeil Island, Jordan stepped onto the ferry to begin his life without bars.

Once back on the mainland, Jordan wasted no time. He continued running, and also dove into professional boxing with the same intensity he had shown on the track. His days were filled with rigorous training sessions, sweat-soaked gym visits, and early morning runs. His dedication to these new pursuits were evident in every muscle of his body.

Jordan also found work immediately, channeling his energy into a job that kept him grounded and focused. It was clear that he would do whatever it took to avoid returning to prison.

Watching him, I realized that, at Jordan's age, the odds were stacked against him. The percentage of those who manage to turn their lives around after incarceration is dishearteningly low. Yet, Jordan's determination, his relentless pursuit of a better life, and his refusal to be defined by his past set him apart. His journey was a testament to resilience and the power of second chances.

'Undeserved favor' is a great working definition of *grace* for me. When I think of my younger brother Jordan, I will always feel like I was undeserving of my relationship with him as a friend and brother. He played the cards he was dealt with remarkable resilience and courage, never once complaining, or showing bitterness. I, on the other hand, was given a few wild cards at my disposal, advantages that I didn't always appreciate. Jordan's life was a complicated grace. He had a way of touching everyone he met, leaving a mark on their hearts. His laughter could light up a room, and his strength was a source of inspiration. Jordan's spirit was a gift; a beautiful, undeserved favor that I will hold close to my heart forever.

Jordan,   JANUARY 21, 2011

I trust that this letter will find its way to you in your new home.
I heard from both Grandma and Ryan that you made it safely. I
will be fascinated to hear from you how the last day at McNeil
went and the transition to the new digs.

Having prayed for you at McNeil these past few months, I now
find that I have had to insert into my prayer, instead of McNeil,
the Progress House. It doesn't flow quite as well yet, but I am
sure it will come with time. I should add, before we completely
let go of McNeil, that your answer to my question regarding
if there'd be anything you'd miss at McNeil was profound. Do
you remember what you said? You stated, "Yes, I will miss
this place because I found my peace here." It was one of those
statements, Jo, that I will forever hold in my heart. I think
in many ways it sums up the maturity of a person when he
or she can say that this place, person, event, etc. which was
poised to minimize me has actually made me stronger. There
is a phrase that appears in the Bible three times—when Joseph
was reflecting on his brothers' attempt to destroy him, when
Esther (who was a Jew) became queen of a foreign land and
wondered about her role in helping her people, and when
Paul was reflecting on the relationship between a master and
a runaway slave who had become a Christian—"for perhaps
such a time as this." The phrase carries in it a capacity to look
over one's shoulder and see all of the things that have taken
place—both good and bad—and conclude that maybe God is
in all of this. I think this statement can be made by anybody,
but it often is not because we refuse to consider that God is in
the tough things of life. You, my young friend, have made this

decision and I trust that you will remember it all of your life.

The poem this week is to help you reflect on the new place you are in and how to make it "home" for the time being. It is called "Boundaries" by (who else?) Mary. I won't go into much detail, but the reason I am sending it is this wonderful phrase, "Where is it? I ask, and then my feet know it. One jump, and I'm home," which I think carries with it the wonderful sense that you are learning (and we are all trying to learn from you) that it is possible by way of our internal compass to be at "home" wherever we jump. I will be praying that, for the time being, Progress House will be your new home.

Your boy, D

Boundaries
By Mary Oliver

There is a place where the town ends
    and the fields begin.
It's not marked but the feet know it,
also the heart, that is longing for refreshment
    and, equally, for repose.
Someday we'll live in the sky.
Meanwhile, the house of our lives is the world.
The fields, the ponds, the birds.
The thick black oaks—surely they are the
    children of God.
The feistiness among the tiger lillies,
the hedges of runaway honeysuckle, that no one owns.
Where is it? I ask, and then
my feet know it.
One jump, and I'm home.

Jordan,

What a surreal week it was with you. To think of how very far away you have felt for a very long time and now to have you walking through the halls of my office on a regular basis. As we have talked about many times before, the one constant in life is that change is always afoot.

With these changes in your situation I have found my prayers changing as well. If I am honest (and here I hope you do not take offense) I have found myself a bit fearful for you. While I know that County, Shelton, and McNeil were no vacation, they were for me a place that felt stable. By stability I suppose I mean that you had a routine, you knew who you were dealing with, and most importantly what to expect. Now as I pray for you I find myself wondering how businesses will respond to you, what these new guards will be like, and will you be able to do those things like exercise that are so important for your mental health. To put it to a bottom line, it was easier to pray for you in the other places than it is in this one. I trust that God will give me new ways to come to peace with this reality.

As a related thought, I think what it comes down to is my deep sense of how cold and cruel this world can be. In a very different kind of way, you have been "protected" from some of these realities. Does this make sense?

With all of this being said, it was great to see you. Your perspective seems very solid in that you know what you are up against, the issues you need to be vigilant around, and what it's going to take to get through it all. I am also very happy that you have had the opportunity to get reunited with your boys, Kris, Nash, and Jeremiah.

The poem that has come to mind this week is one of my favorites called "Stopping by Woods on a Snowy Evening" by Robert Frost. I hope I haven't already sent it to you. Anyway, I thought about it for two reasons. Frost situates the poem in a person who is outside driving his horse along in a snow storm through a village and past a neighbor's house. He states emphatically that "he will not see me stopping here" which is what you would assume he would do. It made me think of you, walking on the streets looking for a job and how you will pass many places that you are familiar with, but won't be "stopping here." I imagine these could be moments that make you rather sad. The poem goes on to describe a few other things, but then gives the reason why this person will not be stopping: "But I have promises to keep, And miles to go before I sleep, And miles to go before I sleep." I don't think, Jo, that I have ever read a more beautiful couple of lines of poetry in my life. The idea that while we would all like to stop and rest a bit, we can't because there are things that we need to get done because of the promises we have made. I hope this encourages you as you take on these next few months.

So from one man who has "miles to go before I sleep" to another man who has "miles to go before he sleeps"—let's you and I keep our promises.

Your boy, D

Stopping by Woods on a Snowy Evening
By Robert Frost

Whose woods these are I think I know.
His house is in the village, though;
He will not see me stopping here
To watch his woods fill up with snow.

My little horse must think it queer
To stop without a farmhouse near
Between the woods and frozen lake
The darkest evening of the year.

He gives his harness bells a shake
To ask if there's some mistake.
The only other sound's the sweep
Of easy wind and downy flake.

The woods are lovely, dark and deep,
But I have promises to keep,
And miles to go before I sleep,
And miles to go before I sleep.

Jo,   **FEBRUARY 4, 2011**

It's been quite a week, has it not? You in T-Town, Egypt at a critical point in its history (have you been following this?), Ryan passing all three of his tests for grad school, and you landing a job. Just a few things to ponder regarding our place in this world and what it all means to live and try to be faithful.

Do you find yourself thinking much about what it means to be faithful? We haven't talked a lot about it and, in some ways, maybe it has been assumed, but it is the essence of what it means to be a follower of Jesus. And while faith can be defined in a lot of different ways, the one I like the best is from one of my favorite theologians (James Alison) who describes it as the "act of relaxing into the struggle."[43] What do you think about that definition? I may have used it in one of my earlier letters, but the reason I bring it up again and the reason it appeals to me is that the definition assumes that faith is: something that we need to do (act), that it acknowledges there is a very real struggle (we both know that, don't we?), and that it ought to manifest itself in a quality of life that is attractive (relaxing). A great example (the greatest, actually) of this "act of relaxing into the struggle" is Jesus. He is the penultimate example of someone who was so confident in who God was that you never see him make a rash move, lose his cool, move more quickly than is required, and seemed to constantly be at peace—even in the midst of horrific realities. I was thinking about a story in the scriptures of him where he was on his way to heal a powerful man's daughter—a power meeting, if you will. As he was headed to his house down a very crowded street, a

---

43 James Alison, *Jesus the Forgiving Victim: Listening for the Unheard Voice* (Glenville, IL: Doers Publishing, 2013).

woman—who had been continuously bleeding for 12 years and had spent all of her money on doctors for a cure that still hadn't come—reached out and touched the edge of his cloak. Instantly Jesus felt his power leave him and she was cured. I should add—all pretty standard stuff. The reason I bring this up, however, is that it says that Jesus "then listened to her whole story."[44] Isn't that remarkable? Here he is on his way to a very important meeting and he still finds time to listen to a marginalized woman's whole story. A perfect example of "an act of relaxing into the struggle"; I hope you have experienced Jesus in this way.

This week I am sending you some random poetic thoughts from none other than your boy, Muhammad Ali. I came across them earlier and instantly thought you would love some of his reflections. Some are so-so, but many are very good. There are three in particular that I like and made me think of you.

The fight is won or lost far away from witnesses—behind the lines, in the gym, and out there on the road, long before I dance under those lights.

A man who views the world the same at fifty as he did at twenty has wasted thirty years of his life.

Service to others is the rent you pay for your room here on earth.

That man was connected! Thanks for reminding me of these and many other truths.

Your boy, D

---

44 Summarization of story told in Matthew 9:20-22, Mark 5:25-34, and Luke 8:43-48

Poetic Quotes[45]
By Muhammad Ali

"I am the greatest; I said that even before I knew I was."

"At home I am a nice guy: but I don't want the world to know. Humble people, I've found, don't get very far."

"The fight is won or lost far away from witnesses—behind the lines, in the gym, and out there on the road, long before I dance under those lights."

"Friendship… is not something you learn in school. But if you haven't learned the meaning of friendship, you really haven't learned anything."

"A man who views the world the same at fifty as he did at twenty has wasted thirty years of his life."

"Service to others is the rent you pay for your room here on earth."

"I never thought of losing, but now that it's happened, the only thing is to do it right. That's my obligation to all the people who believe in me. We all have to take defeats in life."

"I'm so fast that last night I turned off the light switch in my hotel room and was in bed before the room was dark."

---

45 "In His Own Words." n.d. Muhammad Ali Center. https://alicenter.org/meet-ali/in-his-own-words/.

"If they can make penicillin out of moldy bread, they can sure make something out of you."

"It isn't the mountains ahead to climb that wear you out; it's the pebble in your shoe."

"It's just a job. Grass grows, birds fly, waves pound the sand. I beat people up."

"It's the repetition of affirmations that leads to belief. And once that belief becomes a deep conviction, things begin to happen."

"I hated every minute of training, but I said, 'Don't quit. Suffer now and live the rest of your life as a champion.'"

"Float like a butterfly, sting like a bee."

Jordan,   FEBRUARY 11, 2011

I hope this letter finds you well. I should add that these letters "feel" different now that you are back in the city. Whereas in the past these letters (along with my occasional visits) were the primary way that we communicated, now with having the opportunity to see you more often the letters have taken on a different shape. We will see how things continue to proceed and whether these letters continue to be helpful to you.

You made mention in the car the other night that I seemed to be a "bit off" and/or that I had "a lot on my mind." As always, you are a perceptive young man. I am also assuming (am I correct?) that some of your sense of this probably came from my interaction with you and Jeremiah. Is this true? All that to say, yes, I feel as though I am carrying a bit of an extra burden these days with our family, my job, and the world as it is. Regarding our family, it is always a delicate dance. While I am very happy with the way your mother has carried her cross of health-related issues this year, there is always a part of me that wonders how long this current good time will last. I also worry a bit about your brothers and their marriages, principally because I know how much work it requires and the capacity to extend forgiveness that often feels out of reach for any of us. For Ryan, I fear—and I am sure he gets this from me—that his constant worrying will take away from the joy life has to offer. With you... well, I think you can fill in the blanks. I am so thankful you are out, but worry if the "streets" will become attractive to you again. I am, as I stated to you, uncomfortable with how you are managing the house rules at Progress, etc. I think my job and the heaviness you feel there can best be summed up in what Shakespeare said about a particular king in one of his plays when he wrote, "heavy is the head that wears the crown."[46] I have a number of decisions I need to make each day and I am always fearful that I may not be up to the task of deciding judiciously, lovingly, and competently. So there you have it.

In thinking about a poem for you this week I came across a quatrain that Steve Lantry read at Mass last Saturday. In listening to it, I immediately thought about you. A quatrain, by the way, is simply a poem with four lines using the French word for *four*. The primary reason I send it is that so much of what we really want at the bottom of it all (marriage, job, religion, lifestyle, etc.) is to be free. We constantly look for all kinds of things to make us free, but more often than not they enslave us. This little poem suggests that the key to freedom is not keeping score, not worrying about money, and not caring about yourself. Makes great sense to me and it is my prayer for all of us.

Your boy, D

---

46 William Shakespeare, *Shakespeare's Henry IV. Part Second*, eds. Hudson, Henry Norman (Boston, New York, Ginn & Company, 1908) Pdf. https://www.loc.gov/item/08022483/.

Quatrain[47]

By Jalaluddin Rumi

Translation by Coleman Barks

Take someone who doesn't keep score,

who's not looking to be richer, or afraid of losing,

who has not the slightest interest even

in his or her own personality. That person is free.

47 *Open Secret: Versions of Rumi*, trans. John Moyne and Coleman Barks (N.p.: Shambhala, 1999), 116. Copyright © 1984 Coleman Barks and John Moyne. Used with permission.

MISHPACHA REFLECTIONS
To See
By Keilah Fanene, Girlfriend

Jordan… what to say? Our time together was, to use the title of this memoir, a complicated grace in every way. From the moment we met, we knew that what we had was real. Game recognized game. Real recognized real. We knew it, and everyone who knew us knew it too. When we were together, everything was at play—the good, the difficult, the holy, the profane—and through it all we came to the realization that it was all grace, but often complicated. What I will be forever grateful for are the ways in which our relationship allowed for this seeming contradiction and Jordan's capacity to use this contradiction to better be able to "see."

Jordan's superpower was "seeing people" which, interestingly enough, comes from the streets. To "see me" on the streets means we are going to have to square off with each other and potentially fight. You can't hide, look away, disappear: You have done something that needs to be held accountable. You gotta see me! And while Jordan had more than enough of the negative side of this phrase from his time on the streets, he took the phrase and translated it in a decidedly positive way as well. Many were the times that he was quick to "see" someone and "show love" that made me take account of how I chose to engage people in the world who happened to cross my path. Many times we would go out together and he would "see" people who he did not know and greet them as we walked by with a, "Top of the morning" or "How's it going?" People walking in typical Washington-style—eyes down, earbuds in and on a mission to get where they need to go—would stop and return the greeting. He would "see" them and conversations would ensue and random connections were made on the spot! When we were in restaurants, he would "see" the staff and make them part of the experience. He would learn their name, share light conversation, and make sure they knew his gratitude. Watching him really "see" people was something I always felt blessed to witness.

And there was a particular time where he chose to "see" that changed me forever.

My son Jabez had a baseball game and was excited when he found out Jordan was going to be there. Jordan, as only Jordan could, had decided it was time for him to take the next step with Jabez's father. While my son was jumping around with joy, I was silently feeling more and more unsettled and filled with anxiety with each passing second. I shared with Jo all my reservations about him being in a shared space with my son's father. Knowing that he and my ex had the potential to be confrontational and combative and that my own interactions with my ex often ended in heated arguments, felt like a recipe for disaster. He listened to all my anxieties and stresses patiently and afterward somehow calmed me with a kiss on the forehead and a simple, "Baby, everything is going to be okay. I promise." One look in his sky blue eyes and feeling his sincerity while wrapped in his strong hug—hugs that I loved so much—I felt a load come off my shoulders. But still… one never knows.

The entire game, I was on edge. I had no idea what to expect! I had never been in this kind of situation before. I was half watching my son's game and half running horror scenarios of things that could happen between these two men. Jo put his hand on my lap when he'd see my tension rising. He'd remind me that everything was going to be fine. The confidence in the way he said it once again gave me some assurance, so I let it go for a little while and continued cheering for my son and his teammates. In short, Jordan was able to "see" me and, as he saw me, I was able to begin to relax.

When the last inning finished, my stress levels were up again—trying to keep an eye on both Jo and my son's dad to make sure they were safely distanced from each other. After the game, my son found me, and we chatted about his victory. While we were talking, I wound up losing track of Jo and my son's dad and in the next moment all my anxieties reached maximum capacity. I looked up to see Jo making a beeline toward my son's dad. I attempted to make a break and try to stop him but as we all know, those long legs got him where he needed to go, and quickly! I didn't have a chance. I looked on in horror, knowing that this could go one of two ways—really well or horribly bad—and I was betting on the latter. I held my breath and then heard Jordan say, coolly, "Hey, I'm Jordan. I just wanted to come over and say that your son is an incredible baseball player and such a bright young man." A thousand thoughts and doomsday outcomes went through my head in a split second! I thought to myself, "What the hell is he doing?! What's Jabez's dad going to say?" Was Jordan initiating going to be a trigger for something dark and dangerous or a switch for something hopeful and healing? As I started to make my way toward them in case anything popped off it was like watching a movie in slow motion, sitting on the edge of my seat waiting to see what would happen next. A second turned into an eternity. Two seconds became infinity. Then, after what felt like forever, and to my thankful surprise, Jabez's dad smiled and introduced himself, thanked Jo, and shook his hand. They spoke for a short time and then went their separate ways. Jordan, in his indescribable way, was able to "see" my ex!

While Jo and I walked to our cars and Jabez walked with his dad to theirs, I was trying to figure out whether I was pissed off at Jo or not. I shared with him exactly how I was feeling—that I was torn. On one hand, I wanted to be so angry that he dismissed my request to steer clear of Jabez's dad. On the other hand, I was so thankful that he did exactly what he did—took everything head on and put himself out there to have a good first encounter with my son's dad for the sake of Jabez and I. He broke the ice so effortlessly and disarmed any chance of a negative first encounter. In the end I settled with the latter—he was able to "see" me, Jabez, and my ex and throw us a solid that has continued to provide ballast as we move forward.

That encounter is a lesson I reflect on often. It's one of those lessons that stick with you and is constantly on the periphery of your mind. I now often ask myself how do I go about "seeing" others I meet out in public or ones who are close to me? How can I "see" ways to disarm charged situations by creating a space of mutual respect? These are the questions that I have internalized because of that day. It's a good reminder to be fully present and fully ourselves in every moment and to see each other.

Jordan saw people. This was his superpower. He took a phrase that meant one thing on the street (and one he was very familiar with) and made it into something completely different. He saw. He continues to see... So until I "see" you again, *manuia le malaga lo'u pele ma felegi.*

Jordan,

It was good to see you the other night and I am glad you like the quatrain I sent you. Isn't it fascinating how sometimes (maybe most of the time) it is the simplest things that are most profound? Increasingly I am discovering that when I write or say things with an attempt to be clear, precise, and simple, that is usually when people afterwards say things like, "Wow, that was deep," and "How did you get so smart?" It kind of makes me laugh.

It is in fact one of the things that I most admire about the person of Jesus. When you read about him in the Gospels, he is always confounding people (particularly the religious leaders) exactly because he is so elegantly simple. I wish I trusted this a bit more. One of my temptations is to try and act like I am smart.

So it sounds as though you and this girl of interest are a bit of a "thing." Are you excited about this? If so, what is it about her that you are particularly fond of? As you well know, relationships can be tricky things so the more you are able to describe to yourself in clear simple ways what it is that you enjoy about her the better it will go for you two. I am excited for you that you have someone that appears to be a good friend, someone you can trust, and one that shares your view on life.

The poem I am sending you this week builds on the quatrain from last week. I am imagining that one of the things that most appealed to you about the poem last week is the word "freedom." I think you and I are similar in this regard: There is nothing as precious to our sense of life than to be free, and because of your recent experience, who better than you to know what that means. I am also imagining that you have learned something about the idea that to be truly free is not what most people think. For example, I think one of the marvelous things about you over the past few months is that while you were imprisoned you actually became freer. The flip side is you and I know many people who appear to be free (money, job, family, etc.) but actually are enslaved. To that end this poem is called "Emancipation."

I don't know how much you will like this poem (some strange words), but her last line is exactly what I think you get: "Except thyself may be Thine enemy; Captivity is consciousness, So's liberty."

It's all about that sense of our consciousness, is it not? I think about when you and I were in Thailand and how many of the people we met (particularly up in the Akha village) were completely free because of the way they thought about things.

Much love, Jo.

D

Emancipation
By Emily Dickinson

No rack can torture me,
My soul's at liberty
Behind this mortal bone
There knits a bolder one

You cannot prick with saw,
Nor rend with scymitar.
Two bodies therefore be;
Bind one, and one will flee.

The eagle of his nest
No easier divest
And gain the sky,
Than mayest thou,

Except thyself may be
Thine enemy;
Captivity is consciousness,
So's liberty.

Jordan,   **FEBRUARY 25, 2011**

This letter comes to you on a very cold, bright blue-skied, and sunny day. Of course you know all of this, but it is nice to acknowledge such a day in the midst of our often gray and sunless winters.

It was good chopping it up the other night with you when I was taking you back to the Progress House. I don't know about you, but I always find it a great grace to be able to talk about stuff that we mutually care about. Ranging from your crazy-ass brother in Ireland producing videos naked, to Ryan's upcoming test, to the stuff that you and I are both facing in our daily lives. Regarding my life, I will be particularly thankful if you can pray for me. In the next two weeks I have a major fundraising meeting in California and then I am off to Dallas for my president's and board meetings. Pray specifically that I will be able to be clear and engaged for the presentations I must deliver. Although I have done it many times before, it always feels like it's my first time all over again. As a result I get those sweaty palms, butterflies, and other nervous-related issues. While I wish I was a bit calmer I suppose, similar to sports, it's God's way of making sure that I am well prepared. All of that to say, would deeply covet your prayers.

I have continued to think about your deep appreciation of the quatrain I sent you. Have you memorized it yet? Memorizing a few key poems is always a very good thing to do. One of the first that I memorized is where Porsche says to Shylock in *Merchant of Venice*: "The quality of mercy is not strained. It is twice blest: to him who receives it and him who gives it."[48]

I remember when I first read it (and actually watched Al Pacino revive it as Shylock in the film—have you seen it?) and found it to be one of those "words" that I am convinced literally changed me. Ever since hearing it I have attempted to be one of those people who does not "strain" (gives it away freely), believing that not only will the person I am giving it to be "blest," but I will as well.

The poem I am sending you this week is a different take on this same theme. It is called "Enemies" by Wendell Berry. There are a number of themes in this poem that I love. The primary reason is it describes how hard it is to do both what the quatrain and the lines from "Merchant of Venice" encourage us to do. It starts by reflecting on how if we don't want "to become a monster" we must "care what they think," but in the very act of doing that "how will you not hate them?" This rings very close to home for me. It then goes on to say that "love" is the key to our freedom (liberty) which manifests itself in "forgiveness." The result is we become free to such an extent that our former enemies are like "sunlight on a green branch" to us. It then ends with, having thought about them in the beginning we "must not think about them again" except to the degree as "monsters" like ourselves because we are "unforgiving." Doesn't this make great sense? I deeply pray that you and I can be those people who are always forgiving.

Your boy, D

---

48 William Shakespeare, *Merchant of Venice, Act IV, Scene 1* [Boston Ginn & co, 1906] Pdf. https://www.loc.gov/item/unk82065364/

Enemies
By Wendell Berry

If you are not to become a monster,
you must care what they think.
If you care what they think,

how will you not hate them,
and so become a monster
of the opposite kind? From where then

is love to come—love for your enemy
that is the way of liberty?
From forgiveness. Forgiven, they go

free of you, and you of them;
they are to you as sunlight
on a green branch. You must not

think of them again, except
as monsters like yourself,
pitiable because unforgiving.

SPRING

Jo,   MARCH 4, 2011

This letter is going to be short and sweet. I just returned from California from a number of meetings and am headed off to Dallas today for some more meetings. Upon my return I am headed to Arch Cape for vacation so next week's letter won't be happening. I will send you two the following week so we can make sure that "we cover all the weeks" while this season of your life continues to unfold.

I have been thinking a bit of our conversation regarding your "encounter" with the guy at the Progress House. It seems, does it not, that life is full of these unpleasant encounters. I am always sad, but never surprised when these kinds of things come up. So much so that one of the things that I will be preparing myself for in anticipation of next week is people who will inevitably get sideways with me. What to do?

My prayer for you, me, and all of us, in this torn-up, angry, pissed-off world is to be people of peace. In particular, I pray this for you because I am so very afraid that you seem to attract this kind of thing. I am not smart enough to know why this is true, but it seems to come your way. And while it is certainly not all your fault, it does seem that you need, for your own peace of mind, to work through what is your part in the equation. What I hope is that you can experience a deep sense that people are people and that you have the capacity and the responsibility to "handle yourself" regardless of what others do or say. Moreover, you can make these decisions because you have done it before! I will forever remember the time at the Y where you turned away from that kid. It remains, to this day, one of the greatest examples I have ever witnessed of someone demonstrating the Spirit of Christ. I know it wasn't easy, that you have had to live with some "stuff" afterwards, but you did, Jo. Thanks for being strong enough to show me what it means to be this kind of man. It will be one of the images that I carry with me next week.

This week's poem is around this kind of stuff. It is called "Confession." One of the reasons it appeals to me is it describes the "Nazi" within all of us. I think it is this "thing" in you, me, and everyone else, that ends up—if not confessed—creating violence. I pray that you and I will become less "Nazi-like" in our future.

Your boy, D

Confession[49]
By Stephen Dobyns

The Nazi within me thinks it's time to take charge.
The world's a mess; people are crazy.
The Nazi within me wants windows shut tight,
new locks put on the doors. There's too much
fresh air, too much coming and going.
The Nazi within me wants more respect. He wants
the only TV camera, the only bank account,
the only really pretty girl. The Nazi within me
wants to be boss of traffic and traffic lights.
People drive too fast, they take up too much space.
The Nazi within me thinks people are getting away
with murder. He wants to be the boss of murder.
He wants to be the boss of bananas, boss of white bread.
The Nazi within me wants uniforms for everyone.
He wants them to wash their hands, sit up straight,
pay strict attention. He wants to make certain
they say yes when he says yes, no when he says no.
He imagines everybody sitting in straight chairs,
people all over the world sitting in straight chairs.
Are you ready? he asks them. They say they are ready.
Are you ready to be happy? he asks them. They say

---

49 Stephen Dobyns, "Confession," in *Cemetery Nights* (N.p.: Viking, 1987)

they are ready to be happy. The Nazi within me wants everyone to be happy but not too happy and definitely not noisy. No singing, no dancing, no carrying on.

MISHPACHA REFLECTIONS
Mount Tahoma
By Dave Osterhaus, Friend

Two posters of Michael Jordan covered my front door and back entrance windows. As I sat with a young man in my office reviewing transcripts and explaining the details of student life at Mount Tahoma, you could hear numerous students trying to gain entrance into my office. The door handle would rattle, knocks would turn into pounding, and voices could be heard pleading to open the door. As the crescendo built louder than usual, a voice was heard above the din: "Open the door, Mr. O! We know you're in there."

I told the young man I was with that we would continue after I got rid of the scrum which had formed outside my door. As they filtered in, my office became packed with half the basketball team, a few of the football players, and an assortment of students who did not care for the classroom. A smile enveloped Jordan's face. Sitting in the middle, Jordan looked light and free. Julio introduced himself and said, "We heard you were coming to MT!" Jordan looked at me and said, "Yeah, Dave is helping me out." One of them spoke up, "You mean Mr. O." 'Mr. O' was the name given to me by staff and students. "You can't call him Dave," one retorted. In his husky, raspy voice Jordan responded, "I can because I have known him my whole life." While it is nervy and awkward having a student call you by your first name, Jordan was my only exception in my 35 years as a high school counselor.

In college I met my wife, Teresa. Dave Hillis, Jordan's dad, was also going out with a Teresa at the time. We were the two Daves and the two Teresas. Eventually we stood with them in their wedding party and a few months later they stood for us in ours. We all began to set down roots in inner-city Tacoma. Children followed—the Hillis' were blessed with three boys, and we had four to outdo them.

When Jordan was born he was gifted with attributes of both his brothers but enjoyed a little extra. Ultra-competitive from day one, Jordan also exhibited characteristics of neurodiversity. He didn't quite get the essence of jokes and if poked he would respond with strength. One day I heard a loud commotion coming from the basement of the Hillis house. I went downstairs and there was Jordan, fighting both brothers at the same time. The three of them, in future years, were a force to reckon with. Jordan, however, carried with him superhuman strength and a work ethic that could not be equaled. Skilled at all sports and enjoying all competition the house of Hillis was always filled with kids, many looking for a place of love and acceptance. On any given day the cemented backyard would host basketball and wrestling matches.

While Patrick and Ryan found a way to use their inherent intelligence to keep ascending the educational ladder, Jordan started losing pace. Frustration would mount for this young man who saw black and white, good and bad, fair and not fair. He was never one not to voice his opinion. He could lead—quarterbacking the team from the lowest socio-economic, crime-ridden, notorious Hilltop neighborhood of Tacoma all the way to the city-wide championship. He grew in reputation as a young teen who never backed down from anything or anyone. Yet, in the classroom he suffered and spent many a day suspended from school for "wanting fairness." He grew in strength, wisdom, and frustration.

I do not know who contacted who. I always left it out there that I can get your kid into Mount Tahoma and put him/her with the right teachers. Mount Tahoma was the third largest High School in Tacoma and known for being 'the roughest.'

There were two things I had to do before Jordan would be able to transfer to my domain. First, I contacted the principal at Stadium High School. I knew him and had collaborated with him in the early days. But this was no piece of cake. "Coop, I need a favor. Before you suspend Jordan Hillis for the rest of the year, send him to us." He replied, "He's been suspended at least eight times. He gets in fights all the time and there is no reasoning with him. Dave, Jordan is just a bad kid and there is nothing you or I can do." I explained to him my history with Jo and my relationship with his family. "You have nothing to lose," I said.

Tom Shearer, the principal at Mount Tahoma and my boss, would indeed be tougher, but we had a long friendship and strong trust. We had pulled off a lot of stuff in our years and dealt with some high-profile issues. Our goal was simply to help students. At first he was hesitant, but he knew of the Hillis family. He knew the other Hillis boys through various sports endeavors. I told him I had called Coop and he would do it. Despite his pessimism and Coop's recommendation that we should not take him, Tom smiled at me and said, "It's my choice and I say we do it!"

Jordan was in.

I finally kicked everyone out except Julio who was going to show Jo the ropes (i.e. my expectations). I first got to know Julio by convincing the principals to write up an I.E.P. so that he could take care of his dying mother during lunch. He had been suspended numerous times for leaving campus to go home and feed and then 'turn' his mother who suffered from AIDS. He became my assistant. I trusted him just as I trusted Jordan.

I sat down with Tom Shearer, and we opened up his transcript to see how far behind Jordan was. Middle school was a bust— he had been socially promoted. In reading his transcript though I noticed an important truth. In every situation and physical encounter that I had read about, never once did the notes say Jo was the aggressor. I immediately liked him even more. Tom and I put together a transcript for ninth and tenth grade. I had some ideas. It may not make sense to all of the teachers (especially some) but it gave him a chance. Jo said, "Straight up Dave, I really don't think school is my thing, but I am willing to try." When you are trusted enough by Jo, and that is not easily accomplished, he has your back in anything. I knew for the next two years he would let me know if anything was going down. Never one to snitch on anyone but he had a moral code that distinguished right from wrong.

The way to exist as a competent counselor in a school that scared many away, was to learn how to negotiate with teachers and establish trust with the students. Jordan was not here to employ his physical skills. Even though we knew each other well, it was his last chance. All sorts of people were in his corner, but this was it. Were we going to see another Jordan who failed miserably? I put him in all Advanced Placement courses.

Two things that my memory would not let go of. One day, coming by the Hillis house when the boys were little, Teresa told me that Dave was reading the boys some books. I quietly tiptoed down the stairs and two of the boys were fast asleep but Jordan was sitting upright in bed at rapt attention. Jordan was asking his dad questions that seemed astonishing for a little guy. It was then I saw the book by Dickens—Jordan had grown up listening to the classics every night. He had no hope in grade school, and with severe dyslexia he was unable to read. He had gotten kicked out of numerous classes because he refused to read out loud. One day Jordan came upstairs with a large book and exclaimed, "Look I can read." Sure enough he flowed through the words, leaving us all with gaping mouths. "But how…?" He had turned the book upside down. Throw in Tourette syndrome and zero trust in education and Jordan's history was actually explainable.

Jordan has his "word," and that was good enough for me. The teachers I placed him with already had too many students, they were way beyond Tacoma Union guidelines. I begged them. I had to remove one nasty student from Mrs. Tommervick's but it was worth it. These were true educators. Hands-on and they enjoyed and—even more so—*loved* the kids. There was one promise that had to be kept though: One episode with Jordan and I would have to remove him immediately. I was kind of worried, but the respect Jo gave me was an assurance. I explained to Jordan's teachers the heightened anxiety which triggers Tourette syndrome and could set him off. The one major agreement was that Jordan could get a pass and work in my office. The first week I saw him every day, at least four to five classes. But eventually something happened, which was not only unusual, but outright extraordinary. Jordan started liking school.

Jordan,   MARCH 11, 2011

Well, I am finally getting settled back into my office after what
feels like a long time away. I think I mentioned it in my letter
a couple of weeks ago, but in the last three weeks I have been
to the San Francisco area, Dallas, and then the Oregon Coast.
Thanks for praying. I think the trips and what I needed to get
done went fairly well.

I don't know if you heard, but an interesting thing happened
down at Arch Cape. We got there on a Thursday at about 5:00
p.m., had a good meal, and then went to bed. At 3:00 a.m. we
were awoken by a siren, loud speaker, and people knocking
on the door due to a tsunami warning. Long and short of it,
because of the earthquake in Japan they anticipated a tsunami
on the Oregon Coast. As a result, we all had to get in the car
and head to higher ground where we, for about four hours,
waited to see what would happen. Ryan, Tad, and I were
actually going to stay put, but a cop came by and forced us
out. One of the reasons—and I did not know this—is that
a tsunami travels at 400 miles per hour! Isn't that incredible?
Think about it this way—when you fly in a jet somewhere the
average speed of your flight is roughly 500 miles per hour. So
to think that a wave, at a speed a little slower than a jet, is
coming across the ocean toward you… it makes one think a bit
about the fragility of life.

While I was down there I also thought (as I always do) a great
deal about you. In particular I thought about how much you
love the place, that last year you were with us right before you
were arrested, and how much has changed in this last year. I

also thought a lot about you being at this place with us next year, you and I smoking a cigar on the deck, having some scotch, and reflecting on all that has taken place. One of the things that I most respect about you is your fearlessness in facing uncomfortable truths and realities. It is these thoughts that led me to send you this week's poem, which is called "A Ritual To Read to Each Other" by William Stafford. I am even thinking that this, along with all the other poems we have had the chance to share over the past year, might be what we do together at our next time at Arch Cape.

I think you will find this poem to your liking. It begins with something that I know is very important to you, that this life we are involved in is relational. He writes, "If you don't know the kind of person I am and I don't know the kind of person you are a pattern that others made may prevail in the world…" I often think of how many of the very sad things in this world are a result of this simple truth—we don't know each other. The poem moves on to discuss the ramifications of not knowing each other, where a "small betrayal in the mind… a shrug that lets the fragile sequence break." Have you noticed this? I think of the meetings I go to and often it comes down to the smallest things where someone forgets a name, they look away from you when you are talking to them, etc.

But there are two lines that are very convicting for me. I will pick those up in my next letter since I am running out of room.

Much love, D

A Ritual to Read to Each Other
By William Stafford

If you don't know the kind of person I am
and I don't know the kind of person you are
a pattern that others made may prevail in the world
and following the wrong god home we may miss our star.

For there is many a small betrayal in the mind,
a shrug that lets the fragile sequence break
sending with shouts the horrible errors of childhood
storming out to play through the broken dyke.

And as elephants parade holding each elephant's tail,
but if one wanders the circus won't find the park,
I call it cruel and maybe the root of all cruelty
to know what occurs but not recognize the fact.

And so I appeal to a voice, to something shadowy,
a remote important region in all who talk:
though we could fool each other, we should consider—
lest the parade of our mutual life get lost in the dark.

For it is important that awake people be awake,
or a breaking line may discourage them back to sleep;
the signals we give—yes or no, or maybe—
should be clear: the darkness around us is deep.

Jordan,   MARCH 18, 2011

It seemed to me given the fact that I was writing two letters to you back to back and the weightiness of that poem that it was worth pondering a bit longer. So where did I leave off?... Oh yes, the two lines that were particularly convicting for me.

The first is the line where he writes, "I call it cruel and maybe the root of all cruelty to know what occurs but not recognize the fact." Does this line make sense to you? How would you explain it in your words? For me I think about how many times I have seen stuff take place—someone is sad, someone needs help, someone needs to be forgiven, someone needs to be prayed for— and I don't recognize it as a truth. Or stated another way, I see something and am not moved to do something as a result. And I do think he is correct in his assessment, that this reality is the root of all cruelty. It seems to me that you must have witnessed this many times at McNeil and that it is this idea that makes the place so difficult. People, like the guards for example, must see what occurs at the time, but they ignore it as a fact. Is this true? I also think about your current situation at Progress House.

The other line is "for it is important that awake people be awake." Jordan, in my mind this is the great challenge of life on this earth: how to stay awake when everything is trying to make us go to sleep, including ourselves. I think one of the reasons we try to go to sleep is that the world is just too painful, so we numb ourselves with alcohol, drugs, tobacco, television, the list goes on. One of the things I deeply appreciate about you is your courage and fearlessness in being willing to stay awake... no matter how painful it is.

This week's poem is "If Someone Cried in Heaven" by St. Catherine of Siena. She was a mystic who lived in the 1300s. The reason I thought about this was JD's death. It is, in my mind, a very wonderful thought to know that there is a place that awaits us where there will be no more crying and even the thought of it would be considered a joke. I love the idea that JD is experiencing that deep truth.

Much love, D

If Someone Cried In Heaven
By Catherine of Siena

If you cried in heaven, everyone
would laugh

for they would know you were just
kidding.

Jordan,   MARCH 25, 2011

You are receiving a lot of mail from me this week. I hope you don't view it as a bit too much and end up throwing it away!

I was thinking about you last night in light of this being the last letter you will receive from me in March of 2011. The reason I suggest this is it seems to me that March is a particularly important month in your life when you reflect on all that has happened to you in March. Do you agree? Of course all months are important because they help us live in the moment. Life being lived is important, but March seems particular to you—examples? Well of course the first example is that it is your birth month. No small thing to know what month you were born in and what it means. You are a child of what some people have termed is the cruelest month, principally because it vacillates between spring and winter. The second is because the month also involves the death of your beloved JD. I know that I will never be able to think about this month in the same way. I still remember—in fact I have it permanently tattooed on my mind—the picture of you two sitting down by the court of the state basketball tournament three days before his death. Clearly you had somehow talked him into sneaking down to this "courtside seat" with you. You probably bribed him with some food! The other date in March is St. Patrick's Day. I have deeply appreciated how you and your brothers have all valued your Irish heritage. What do you think? Is this a very strong case for March being a critical month for you?

This week's poem is called "The Three Goals" by David Budbill. I have not read any of his poetry other than this one, but liked what I read, specifically (and this is the way my mind works when reading poetry) how it made me think of you. I have said this many times before to you, but you do this "first goal" well where you "see the thing itself in and for itself." I have watched you many, many times describe something not for what we want it to be, but for what it is—this is a rare gift. The "second goal," the poet states, is to see "each individual thing as unified." I think you are working on this. Sometimes it still seems to me that you have a way of seeing things in black and white (the first goal), but then not seeing how they can all connect. Do you think I am correct in this assessment? And then finally there's the "third goal," which the poet admits none of us get. You and I can both keep working on this one together. I know I will need your help.

I look forward to seeing you at Mike and Kathy's tomorrow. It has been enjoyable to have you be the reason that the Hillis family is able to gather on a regular basis.

Your boy, D

The Three Goals
By David Budbill

The first goal is to see the thing itself
in and for itself, to see it simply and clearly
for what it is.
    No symbolism, please.

The second goal is to see each individual thing
as unified, as one, with all the other
ten thousand things.
    In this regard, a little wine helps a lot.

The third goal is to grasp the first and the second goals,
to see the universal and the particular,
simultaneously.
    Regarding this one, call me when you get it.

Jordan,

Good morning, my young brother! As has been my custom for the past year on Friday mornings, I am sitting at my desk, listening to my monks, burning incense, praying for you as I write this short letter, and thinking about what poem I might send you. Vernon Grounds stated the following that shapes my Friday morning ritual with you: "Will our habits be mere ruts of routine? Or will they become "grooves of grace?"[50] I am happy to report the routine of writing to you has become a "groove of grace." My suspicion is that you have these as well. I would add, however, that while I see quite clearly your "ruts of routine"—exercise, reading, loyalty to friends—I would be interested to know where you experience the "grooves of grace." Does anything come to mind?

I have been feeling a bit heavy this week. I am not fully certain all that is contributing to this, but I feel it nonetheless. I think some of it has to do with having dinner with Nana and Ryan on Wednesday and being struck at how quickly she is aging. I also found myself wrestling with a deep sense of failure when it comes to my prayer life. Namely, I think about all things I pray for and, if I am honest, see how few of these prayers are answered. It raises a number of questions ranging from: Am I praying for the wrong things? Is there something in me that prevents God from acting on my behalf? Is there a God? Do you have moments like this? If so, what do you do about them? I am confident that somehow and in some way God will show up, but it is the shits going through it. Any wisdom

---

50 "Grooves Of Grace." 2006. Our Daily Bread. https://odb.org/2006/02/21/grooves-of-grace.

on this matter you might have to share with me would be deeply appreciated.

This of course leads me to my poem for the week and, you guessed it, I am going to my homerun-hitter, Mary. This poem is called simply (and interestingly enough) "Praying." It is such an uncomplicated little poem that one almost misses the huge ideas that sit within it. As always with her, I love that she starts her poem with what already is—"blue iris… weeds in a vacant lot… few small stones." I think I have said this to you before, but I like this quality above all other qualities in a poet—the ability to see what is already going on. She then goes on to state that our job is to "pay attention and patch a few words together." This simple reflection provides immense freedom for me. I am embarrassed to say how often I am inattentive and, ironically, I am so because I am so busy trying to figure out how to pray. She goes on to state that "this (and by this she means prayer) isn't a contest, but the doorway into thanks, and a silence in which another voice may speak." What a fantastic line and oh, so convicting. I always compete, even in things like prayer that I have no control over. So I hope and pray that you and I will be able to enter into the "doorway of thanks, and a silence in which another voice may speak."

As always Jo, my deepest love, respect, and appreciation for you,

D

Praying
By Mary Oliver

It doesn't have to be
the blue iris, it could be
weeds in a vacant lot, or a few
small stones; just
pay attention, then patch

a few words together and don't try
to make them elaborate, this isn't
a contest but the doorway

into thanks, and a silence in which
another voice can speak.

MISHPACHA REFLECTIONS
All-City
By Dave Osterhaus, Friend

The teachers at first seemed agitated that I put Jordan in their courses—and not just any courses, but the toughest ones we had. One teacher, Mrs. Tommervick, came in every day and said, "I like Jordan and he is quiet but I am overwhelmed." I asked her to stay the course, believing something good was happening.

Sometimes students start clowning on each other and the intensity rises to a boiling over. Jordan, streetwise and self-assured, also loved the game of "talking trash." One day, there was a knock at my office door. It was Emmanual, all 6'6" of him. I have known him since he played soccer with my son in grade school. He saunters into my room and asks, "You know the new kid in our class?"

"You mean Jordan? Yes, I know him very well."

"Well, I told you I would say something when I am involved with something. I do want to graduate."

"Ok, I'm all ears," I said.

He continued, "I am going to beat him up as soon as the bell rings."

I smiled. "You trust me, Emmanual?"

"I do, that's why I am telling you."

I moved in close and with a half-whisper I said, "You are not going to beat him up. If you fight Jordan Hillis, he will literally tear you apart. Sorry to be so graphic but I know him, and he is the toughest guy I know or have ever known. Here is what you are going to do: Go back to the classroom and apologize to him. Do not worry about your pride. Nobody in Tacoma would mess with him. Please, do what I told you. Your rep will be solid and you will gain a friend who will have your back."

Emmanual went back to the classroom, apologized in front of everyone, and Jordan gave him his hand.

Jordan did not just thrive but earned almost straight A's. The questions raised by the worried teachers were long forgotten. In what seemed like the blink of an eye, Jordan rarely visited me during class. I walked by a few of his classes and there he sat, in the front row. Teachers would tell me that having Jordan in the class was the best thing to happen. Instead of going to Mr. O's he would quiet the gregarious and disruptive students. With Jo entrenched right next to the teachers, students began following his example. Each of the teachers were master teachers, exhibiting hands-on lessons and operating at the highest educational level. Jordan drank from the realization that he was learning.

One day Mrs. Tommervick came to my office. I saw the tears start falling to the ground. I could not understand her. She mentioned Jordan and my first response was, "It finally happened." My heart broke. But she corrected me immediately and wept as she told me, "In the beginning I was hard and didn't understand, but Jordan is now my favorite. He knows the classics almost by heart. He is the reason I am having the best year of my career. And by the way, he just won the all-city poetry contest!" Needless to say, we shared a tear together.

There is so much more I could write. Jordan was blessed with obstacles that made him unique and exquisite. My two years with Jordan were the highlight of my career. Jordan was kind, deliberate, thought-provoking, and when he said he would do something it was always spectacular. Jordan Hillis changed my life and I will never be the same without him.

Jordan,   APRIL 8, 2011

Another week… they do keep moving, don't they? I was thinking
the other day that while I will rejoice with you and others when
your "time" is officially up, I will miss writing these letters to
you. They have had the net effect of tethering my soul to God's
command of time, the ordering of things, and our small part
in it all. Whether you know it or not (and I almost hesitate to
write it) your incarceration has had some gifts it has given to
me. Maybe with your entry into the service (that I know we are
both praying for) I will figure out some way to continue to do
something like this. What do you think?

I wanted to tell you that I deeply respect and also think you are
being very wise in your decision regarding your relationship
and the girl you were dating. These matters of the heart—who
we love, why we do so, what does it mean, etc.—have to be
navigated carefully. All too often people make decisions about
those things that matter most, carelessly. I perceive that you
have spent time thinking through your future, your and her
current status, and other related realities, and have come to
a very solid decision. You also made mention that you "aren't
sure you are very good at deciding such things." The truth
about that is nobody is very good at those kinds of things. In
the end we simply need to make these decisions with as little
violence as possible and trust God with the future. All that to
say, mad respect for the way you have and are handling this.

The poem I am sending you this week is a further reflection
on some of my thoughts above. The poem is called "Sitting by
a Bush in Broad Sunlight" by Robert Frost (I have sent you a

couple of his poems). There are a number of reasons I like it. You may or may not know this, but it is (at least from my perspective) a reflection on a story in the Bible where Moses encounters God in a burning bush and receives instructions to free the Israelites from the Egyptians. Do you know this story? Anyway, it is my suspicion that Frost read or at least was familiar with the story, and in some ways longed (like we all do) for a direct encounter with God, but was honest enough to realize most of us don't have one. Maybe stated more simply: How do you continue to believe in the existence of God and at the same time have what appears to be so little actual contact? I think this is what he means when he starts the poem by writing, "When I spread out my hand here today, I catch no more than a ray to feel of between thumb and fingers; No lasting effect of it lingers." Man, have I experienced that a few times. In the next two stanzas he makes an argument for why there is "no lasting effect," but then moves to the fourth and fifth where each one begins with God. In the fourth he perfectly captures what I think God has done, where he "declared he was true, And then took the veil and withdrew." It is thoughts like this that have helped me better understand the silence of God. Not the absence, but the silence. This is one of the reasons why I go to the monastery. In the fifth stanza he comes to his great conclusion where he still declares God's existence, but only knows of it in two fundamental forms: "our breath" and "our faith."

I hope this reflection helps you with decisions like the one you made about your relationship, as well as others moving into the future: that we need to do what we are able to do (breath) and also trust God with the results (faith).

Much love, D

Sitting by a Bush in Broad Sunlight
By Robert Frost

When I spread out my hand here today,
I catch no more than a ray
To feel of between thumb and fingers;
No lasting effect of it lingers.

There was one time and only the one
When dust really took in the sun;
And from that one intake of fire
All creatures still warmly suspire.

And if men have watched a long time
And never seen sun-smitten slime
Again come to life and crawl off,
We not be too ready to scoff.

God once declared he was true
And then took the veil and withdrew,
And remember how final a hush
Then descended of old on the bush.

God once spoke to people by name.
The sun once imparted its flame.
One impulse persists as our breath;
The other persists as our faith.

Jordan,

Greetings my brother and, I should add right from the outset, my mind is still reeling from the conversation we had in the car yesterday.

Specifically, your reflections on the texture of mercy and the ways it does and doesn't work. You asked some very good questions and made some very significant statements. The one that was hardest to hear, in part because I am afraid it is partly true, was, "You can't show mercy in the world or you will be eaten alive." Yikes!

You surfaced something that has hounded me all of my life, where I have searched for answers and, I am afraid to say, I am not sure I have any. I know what I want to believe about this issue, that turning the other cheek, forgiving, being willing to walk away, etc. is the way to go and that it works. But time after time in my life I have seen just the opposite. Like you, I have been "eaten alive" as a result of believing in the power of mercy. For example, I am currently in a situation where I sense there is a particular individual that I work with that is taking advantage of me and Leadership Foundations precisely because of the grace and the mercy that I have extended to him. I find myself getting evermore angry (I think this may be where some of your anger issues come from—namely me) and wanting to do something about it. What is interesting is that I am equally angry at him for taking advantage of me, but also angry at myself for allowing it to happen. Have you experienced this? And so I ask myself, what does mercy look like in this situation and should I even be looking for it?

But I also have this longing in me to believe in mercy. What, for example, would this world be like without it? I know you might answer this question by saying, "It would look exactly like it does," but don't you think that even in the midst of all of this horrible stuff we do in fact experience an "abode of mercy" as the poet Denise Levertov writes? This is what I want to believe Jo, that there is mercy in this world and that you and I can somehow be a part of the process of making it a reality. Lord knows I do not know how to do it, but I am going to continue to try even if it means the death of me (which is probably what it will come to).

So here is the poem this week—a section from *The Merchant of Venice*. I think it speaks for itself. With you, I am committed to trying to figure this out.

Much love, and again, thanks for the conversation. D

The Merchant of Venice, Act 4, Scene 1
By William Shakespeare

The quality of mercy is not strained,
It droppeth as the gentle rain from heaven
Upon the place beneath. It is twice blest:
It blesseth him that gives and him that takes.
'Tis mightiest in the mightiest; it becomes
The throned monarch better than his crown.
His scepter shows the force of temporal power,
The attribute to awe and majesty,
Wherein doth sit the dread and fear of kings;
But mercy is above this sceptered sway,
It is enthroned in the hearts of kings;
It is an attribute to God himself;
And earthly power doth then show likest God's,
When mercy seasons justice. Therefore, Jew,
Though justice be thy plea, consider this:
That in the course of justice none of us
Should see salvation: we do pray for mercy,
And that same prayer doth teach us all to render
The deeds of mercy.

Jordan,

Well here I am writing to you on Good Friday, which is a part of something called the *Triduum* (Latin for three days)—Maundy Thursday, Good Friday, and Easter Sunday. I don't know how much you remember or whether or not I even shared much with you and your brothers (one of the things that haunts me a bit... did I ever really share anything at all with you guys about Jesus?), but these are the days that Christians celebrate Jesus dying for our sins.

On Maundy Thursday, Jesus was betrayed by Judas and denied by the 11 others (he had 12 disciples in all). While it is always heartbreaking to reread this story, I am thankful for it in that I am reminded of the relevance of Jesus' story. You and I have talked a lot about this issue—people not having each other's back. There is nothing that is more difficult for me to bear than when I feel like I am betrayed or, even worse, when I am the betrayer (which I have been in lots of tiny ways). More than money, failure, struggle, and a whole host of other things—betrayal is the worst. In the midst of that, Jesus (and this is what Maundy Thursday pivots around) bends down and washes these very betrayers' feet to show them what real leadership means. I don't know about you, but could you muster up the courage and strength to wash someone's feet who you know is going to betray you?

Today, on Good Friday, Jesus officially dies on the cross. There's lots of stuff in this story... people spitting on him, pulling his beard, giving him vinegar to drink, etc. The most striking thing for me, however, is when Jesus on the cross says, "My God, my

God, why have you forsaken me?"[51] Similar to the relevance of the betrayal in Maundy Thursday, here I find a deep resonance to feeling forsaken. For example, I know I love God, but there are many times when I feel forsaken by God. I am so very thankful that in some strange way this is something that God understands.

Then of course Holy Saturday combines with Easter. That very simple fact that in Easter we know that death, defeat, shame, and all the other stuff that we struggle with doesn't have the last word... well, that's what it is all about, Jo.

Thanks for letting me get a bit of "my preach" on. This poem this week is simply by a friend, Dr. Andy Anson, called "Holy Saturday."

Much love, D

---

51 Matthew 27:46, ESV

Holy Saturday[52]
By Dr. Andy Anson

You are a mystery to me
And yet you are the most familiar of the week—
The dark hours between The Night and The Morning
When our souls whisper: "Where are you?"

We'd grown used to seeing you walk in our midst
And your words, though riddled with the unknown,
    brought with them a peace.
Even your posture of pain is one we've grown to see as love—

But now the wood is bare.
The chapel is quiet, and I don't know where to place you;
And so, like every night, I wonder:
"Do you hover just over my shoulder while I'm bent in prayer?
"Is that you that stirs the dark air?
"Or are you locked inside the cold chambers of the heart,
    waiting for me to roll the stone?"

---

52 Used with permission

MISHPACHA REFLECTIONS
Two Deaths
By Patrick Hillis, Brother

Death #1

When our cousin JD died at the age of eight, I was 13, Ryan was 11, and Jo was barely 10. Jo and JD were inseparable, cousins by blood but best friends and brothers by choice. The night before JD died, he and Jo slept over at our Nana's house, which was Jo's birthday wish that year. On Sunday they were back at our place, enjoying a sunny day playing basketball in the backyard with Ryan and I. Uncle Mark arrived to visit before taking JD home. Shortly after Mark's arrival, JD started complaining of a headache—what we later discovered was an aneurysm beginning to burst in the beautiful boy's brain. JD left the basketball court and went to the kitchen for a glass of water, where he collapsed and was found by my mom. Mom let out a shriek and called for help, Mark came running, scooped JD into his arms and raced to his blue Datsun where they piled in and sped off to the hospital. My brothers and I looked on, stunned by what was unfolding.

Jordan, Ryan, and I tried to make sense of what was happening as we were left alone to hear from the adults about JD's status at the hospital. When Mom and Dad returned later that night, we were told JD wasn't doing well but the doctors were doing everything they could to help him. Though I felt reassured by this, Jo knew something wasn't right. Jo always had an uncanny sense for identifying when something wasn't right, either within a situation or with a person.

The next day, Ryan and I went to school feeling scared and unsettled. Jordan refused to go and said he would instead go to the hospital with Mom and Dad. A couple hours into the day, Ryan and I were called to the school office over the intercom, where we found Mom looking shook up. Once we got in the car, she shared we were off to the hospital where JD was on life support and unlikely to survive. When we arrived at the hospital, we saw a room full of our community, surrounding Uncle Mark and Aunt Cheryl as they sobbed and looked like they were physically being held upright. JD was not going to make it. I remember looking for my dad and finding him sitting against the waiting room wall, audibly crying with his head against his knees. I had never seen him cry before.

We were brought into JD's room to say goodbye. Ryan stood against the wall looking out the window in disbelief. I went to the foot of the bed and started talking (as a born verbal processor I couldn't help myself). As I started to say how I loved him and was so sad this was happening, Jordan cut me off with sharp words and painful wails. He crawled onto the bed next to JD, yelling at God that this wasn't supposed to be happening. Jo was pleading with God aloud for all to hear, that this should be him and not JD, that he desperately wanted to trade places. At the age of 10, Jordan understood something that I couldn't comprehend at the age of 13. This tragic passing would shape him profoundly and there was no point at which he would ever fully recover. I was naive, not grasping the magnitude of what was taking place.

JD's death marked the beginning of our family's lifelong journey with grief. Jordan understood and was changed by it. In a new way, he began to see life through a lens that first and foremost recognized unfairness in the world, and he developed an inability to accept inequality or injustice in any form.

As the poet Leonard Cohen once said, "There is a crack in everything, that's how the light gets in."[53] This encounter with death gave Jordan a particular view of these cracks in our world, and a profound sensitivity to the light they let through. He wrestled beautifully with this metaphor throughout his life, relentlessly pointing out cracks and light.

Death #2

Jo died in the parking lot of a restaurant in Yakima, WA, a ten-minute drive from the drug rehab facility he was to be admitted to an hour later. About a year before his death, Jordan was salmon fishing on a boat in Alaska where he sustained a nearly fatal injury. In the months to follow, he went on to have multiple operations and was largely immobile, relying on prescribed pain medication and the people around him to care for his daily needs. A few months later he worked his way back to walking on his own, but would often resort to using painkillers and cocaine to treat the ongoing physical and emotional pain he experienced, even after the prescriptions were unavailable. In the weeks leading up to his death, Jordan was depressed in a way I have never seen. He was clouded by drug use and, in my view, didn't want to die but wasn't sure about living.

After weeks of waiting for the results of a court-ordered drug evaluation, we received a recommendation on September 7th

---

53 Leonard Cohen, "Anthem." Track 1 on *The Future*, Columbia, 1992.

for him to attend a 30-day inpatient program. Earlier that morning, I had gotten a call from my parents saying that Jordan had taken a bad fall the night before and had been resting in their bed since around 4 a.m. So I hurried over after dropping my kids off for their first day of school. When I walked in the room, I saw Jo in mom and dad's bed, looking like he had been on the wrong end of a brawl the night before. When he saw me he greeted me as he often would, "Whadddup, P?"

I replied, "Whaddddup, my guy. You look miserable. What can I do to help you?"

"Let me rest and I'll be looking better than you, as usual."

"You hungry for one of my famous salami sandwiches?" I asked.

He said, "Yes, please, my brother."

I whipped it up—sharp cheddar and salami on sourdough, pure and perfect, just how Mom made them. We were raised on salami. I brought it to him and sat on the bed while he enjoyed it. He told me, "You still got it, P." I told him we just got his drug eval results back and I was gonna find him a place to get better. He nodded and went back to sleep. I went to the other room and started making calls. I probably made 10 before finding a place he could go that day. The place was three hours away and they would hold a bed for five hours. Dad and I got Jo up and walked him to the car. Jo was in the back, D drove, and I rode shotgun.

Once we got going, Jo began making calls, announcing to his ex-wife, girlfriend, and a few close others that he was off to rehab, was ready to get better and would see them in a month. As we continued driving, Jo mentioned he was prepared to go but wouldn't do so unless we stopped for a quick bite to eat before dropping him off. This seemed reasonable, but served as a reminder that this thing was delicate and his going to the rehab program was voluntary. We were tight on time but would be able to stop for 30 minutes and still get him there with room to spare.

When we got to the restaurant the conversation was candid and tense. Jo explained he was resigned to go to rehab but wanted us to know that what we thought were his drug induced hallucinations in the previous weeks were actually real. He had people and spirits out to get him, make no mistake about it. Jo excused himself to use the bathroom. D and I looked at each other and knew it was time to make moves.

Jo returned and was in a newly altered state of mind. He had definitely gone to the bathroom to use cocaine. He came back to us and could basically only walk with assistance. He was speaking loudly and somewhat incoherently, telling me he could do 30 days of rehab like a day at the beach. We escorted him towards the car as he stumbled. Right as we got to the car with the door open, he had a massive seizure and collapsed to the ground as dad and I did our best to catch him and lay him on the concrete. We quickly grabbed a pillow from the car and put it behind his head while I called 911. As Jo convulsed on the ground we saw his sockless feet getting bloodied by rubbing on the hot cement—my dad grabbed a blanket and put it below them. The ambulance was there within minutes, quickly stabilizing Jo whose seizure had stopped. With an IV line in place and now on a stretcher, the medic told us he was stable and they would transport him to the hospital. I grabbed Jo's shoulder and told him hang in there, we would be right behind the ambulance.

Quickly, I called the rehab facility to see if we could delay his admittance by a day, while my dad worked on finding us a place to stay for the night. Moments later, I could see commotion at the back of the ambulance. Something wasn't right. I called my dad over. Jordan had lost his pulse and they were now performing chest compressions and administering drugs in an attempt to revive him. This went on for 40 minutes while we looked on from the rear of the rig. They could not bring him back. We were invited to enter the ambulance and say our goodbyes.

We sat there stunned. Our guy had passed to the other side. What the fuck?! Not like this. We had so much more to do.

D and I looked at one another, what now? Stay? Drive home? We drove home, first calling Ry and Mom. Ry needed to know first. Mom needed Ry there when she heard. We then called a list of everyone dear to Jo: his ex-wife, his girlfriend, his closest friends… one by one. They all had wildly different responses… anger, tears, screaming. Some spoke frantically and wanted all the details, others groaned or remained silent. D drove. I rode shotgun.

When we arrived back in Tacoma, I will never forget what we experienced. Our family and friends—the mishpacha— were there, waiting for us in the street as we pulled up to the condo. Neither of us opened the car doors. The mishpacha did. Waiting to embrace us. Waiting to hear more details. Waiting to mourn with us.

On our drive over earlier that day, one of the things I talked with Jo about was all the stuff I was excited to do with him and our kids once he got out of rehab: Sounders games, Mariners games, park visits etc. His response in the moment was, "I love that, P. I can hardly wait to get back and get to it. But don't wait for me… go get my kids while I'm gone. It means the world to me knowing you're thinking of them and including them in your adventures." At the time, neither of us knew it would be longer than 30 days, but his command to go be with his kids remains.

Since then, I think of that final conversation between Jo and I every day, looking for cracks and light. I mostly don't find it, but sometimes I have spotted a glimmer and like to think it could be Jo on the other side, shining through a crack and saying, "Whadddupp, P?"

I experience these two deaths as inextricably linked. JD and Jordan, separated with the first death and reunited with the second. I learned to grieve with JD's passing, in large part watching how Jordan did. With Jordan's death, I find myself feeling defeated, feeling like I failed my little brother. In the end, I wasn't able to help him weather the incredible storm he experienced, both within himself and in navigating the circumstances of his life. My brother was haunted most of his life, and in many ways, this began with the death of JD. Throughout our lives together, Jordan's mental health journey was painful and yet incredibly inspiring to witness. The way he battled made me proud. He was a poet, and a warrior. A beautiful soul who was never quite welcomed or at home in this world. A complicated grace to behold.

Jordan,   APRIL 29, 2011

It was good to see you—even for a brief minute—this morning. It always encourages my soul when I see you planning the day in front of you and it includes something like running the Five Mile Drive with your brother. In short it is a significant answer to prayer for me in that it means: you and Ryan are good friends, you are serious about your health, you are an athlete. I am hoping to get to the Y myself sometime today.

Although this feels like a bit of a refrain, it is worth noting again—I can't believe how quickly time is moving as it relates to you and that this letter signifies the end of April. You are now less than two months away from having this entire episode behind you.

I wanted to take a bit of a risk and let you know that I am praying every day for your admission into the military. The reason that it is a bit of a risk is that I am afraid my prayers for you and your brothers may set up a set of expectations. On the one hand, I want you to deeply believe in God and that God answers prayer, that you can make your requests known to God (whatever they may be) and fully expect God to answer your prayers because there is nothing God wants to do more than give you the desires of your heart. I also must admit that in believing this truth myself I have had many prayers that were not answered and that has made me question whether or not God is on my side. Thus my fear, stated very plainly as a question: Should I encourage you, me, and others, to make requests in prayer fearing that if they are not answered the way we want it will cause unbelief in God? Does this make sense?

For example, along with praying that you gain admission into the military, I am also praying that Ryan will get accepted into grad school (we will find out this Monday), and that Patrick will land a good job once he has finished his MBA in Ireland. In some sense I want to say this to each of you on the front end so that, upon getting the good news, each of you will be able to have further confidence that God is real, alive, and good. And of course just the opposite is true as well. I trust somehow that in showing you the inner-workings of this kind of thinking I will somehow encourage your own life of faith.

This of course leads to the poem this week, interestingly enough about prayer and one that I think I have already sent you—"Praying" by Mary Oliver. In short, she says the key is to "pay attention" and "be thankful" which is what I will continue to work on with you and others.

Your boy, D

Praying
By Mary Oliver

It doesn't have to be
the blue iris, it could be
weeds in a vacant lot, or a few
small stones; just

pay attention, then patch
a few words together and don't try
to make them elaborate, this isn't
a contest but the doorway

into thanks, and a silence in which
another voice can speak.

Jordan,

In sending you this letter I am also aware that I think I may be seeing quite a bit of you with what it sounds like will be two days off. I am particularly glad that you will be able to join us on Mother's Day. I know it will mean a lot to your mom.

I have been thinking a bit about your latest "encounter" with your drug counselor—nasty stuff. I am never surprised but always a little bit sad when I hear of stories like this. It seems that power in the hands of humans, more often than not, moves to some bad places. Of course what makes it even more complicated is that we all recognize we need it to get things done.

With that being said, and reflecting on your situation, it does move me to ask the question: What should our response be in the face of someone like the person you are describing who is abusive? Should we fight back? Should we turn the other cheek? Should we ignore? Should we run away? I honestly don't know, Jo. I should also add that it is one of the parts of Jesus that is most perplexing to me. At times he seems to employ all of what I just described, so then the question becomes: How does one know when to do which?

Increasingly I am trying to recognize three things in my response to the abuse of power which then helps me decide what to do. The first is that no matter how much of a bastard I think that person is, he or she is a creation of God. The second is that I am as capable as anyone to be abusive with power. The third, and quite possibly the most difficult, is that whatever I do it must have forgiveness and reconciliation as its motive.

This of course raises an interesting question for someone like you: Is it possible to fight back and be motivated by forgiveness and reconciliation? I actually think it is. This is a bit of the reason why I want you to read about the life of Bonhoeffer because this was the great fight in his life. How could he, as a Christian who believed in love and forgiveness, decide to try and kill someone? I think you will find it very intriguing.

Well enough of the sermon. This week's poem is one that I am sending simply because I like it. It is by Meister Eckhart. I won't say much about it. I will be very interested in knowing what you think.

Your boy, D

He Told Me a Joke
By Meister Eckhart

My Lord told me a joke.

And seeing Him laugh has done more for me
than any scripture I will
ever read.

Jordan,

Greetings my brother and as always, I trust and pray that this letter finds you well. If my math is right I now have seven letters left to write before you are free. That is a staggering thought. I have wondered whether or not this time would ever come.

This week my thoughts have run toward conversations you and I have had (as well as experiences) of feeling accused, condemned, and judged. For whatever reason I have been acutely aware of how often judgment—me toward others and others toward me—happens. It sometimes appears that we almost don't even know how to behave without judgment. In whatever we do we seem to need to decide that we are better and they are worse. And as much as I hate to see it take place between people, I also have to admit that this spirit is very much alive in me.

Do you feel this tension? I have often wondered if this reality increases or decreases in prison. What is your sense of that? One of the things that has always encouraged me about you and your brothers is what appears to be the lack of judgment that you three display toward others. Very early in your lives you each demonstrated what it means to be able to celebrate another person's success. I should also add that this was one of the things that I have always appreciated about the city versus the suburbs. I remember distinctly watching people cheer you on as you quarterbacked the Hilltop Oilers and Cowboys. Not that there weren't some haters, but by and large they were on your side in a way that I never witnessed on other teams. Do you remember it that way?

It is in light of these thoughts I am sending you something I was asked to write. The context is Bishop Tutu from South Africa spoke this past week at the Tacoma Dome around the theme of what makes for peace. Some people wanted to put a magazine together to celebrate his coming and also get people thinking about this issue. I was one of the people they asked. I have enclosed the article I wrote and would love to know what you think. Much of what I wrote in it was shaped and influenced by what I hope for you and your brothers as well as the way you have lived this truth out.

Much love, Jo. D

The Finger
By Dave Hillis

Nothing haunts people's sense of peace more than the memory of being pointed out by a finger. Whether it was a teacher pointing for an answer we did not know, an authority figure pointing a finger to come, or someone close pointing out a deficiency—all bring a corresponding amount of shame and lack of peace.

My most dominant memory of finger pointing was my 7th grade basketball coach. We were trying out for a basketball team that involved three days of practices where skills, temperament, and athletic ability were scrutinized by him. On the final day we were lined-up against the gym wall and he pointed his finger to one of two places: the "A team" where brand new uniforms awaited, or the "B team" where we would languish for eternity in basketball mediocrity. It was an example of one of the most unfortunate uses of "finger pointing" that I have experienced.

"Finger pointing" carries over into our spiritual lives. This comes from the perception that God sits in the heavens ever accusing us with a long slender finger by etching into granite the laws that find us forever guilty—an eternal "B team" of existence, if you will. We wrestle with this notion that we have been accused by the very finger of God—forever damned and ultimately condemned. But there is another "finger of God" that shows up in our reflection—Jesus writing on the ground with a woman accused by "other fingers."

The teachers of the law and the Pharisees (the other fingers) bring before a crowd a woman caught in adultery. They ask Jesus about the finger of God in the Law of Moses and whether he agrees to its pointing—a death sentence for the woman. Jesus, in one of those moments caught for eternity, bends down in the dirt and begins to write with his finger. The scripture never makes clear what Jesus writes, but he interrupts his soiled essay with the simple statement, "He who is without sin, let him be the first to throw a stone at her."[54] And with that, the other fingers begin to walk away, leaving a finger writing in the ground the new commandment of God—no condemnation and, as a result, peace.

The story never tells us how it ends; but imagine how this woman walked back out into the world knowing the fingers were gone and the peace she felt? Imagine how you might make for peace in this city with no sense of condemnation?

Practice

When you pray today, reflect on the ways that you have sensed "fingers" pointing at you and how they make you feel and the obstacles they have created in your prayer life. Now imagine the finger of God that neither condemns nor accuses, but points only in order to bless. How might that make a difference?

---

54 John 8:7, NASB

Jordan,   MAY 20, 2011

Well, here I sit on a very beautiful afternoon preparing to leave my office. Of course I couldn't do so without my letter to you. It just wouldn't feel right no matter how nice the weather is outside.

In writing my letter last week and noting how little time we now have in front of us, I failed to inform you that the plan with this last bunch of letters is to try and articulate to you the gift you have given me over the past 15 months. I have hinted at this idea in some of my other letters and some of the poems I have sent you (remember Mary's poem on "Uses of Sorrow"?), but I have not directly stated it. So by way of articulating to you over these next few weeks things that I have learned that have changed me, let me begin with a metaphor.

Have you ever heard the old adage, when life gives you lemons, make lemonade? If I have heard it once I have heard it a thousand times, ranging from Hallmark cards, to sermons, to other trite bits and pieces of advice. But here's the deal—it seems to me that more often than not lemons just won't turn into lemonade—feel me? So then what do you do? It seems there are two choices (that at least I have witnessed): You either begin to make artificial lemonade or you begin to avoid certain lemon groves altogether. I should add, parenthetically, that I used this image once in a talk I had to give and a musician went and made a song out of it. I have the CD if you ever want to get with it. This has led me to wrestle with this idea: Could it be that there is redemption in the lemon itself apart from whether it turns into something "good"? Well, that's my suspicion and one that your last 15 months has taught me in ample measure.

Putting it very simply, but also very carefully because of what you have gone through: I discovered that I didn't need to wait for you to get out of prison or learn some great lesson from it (although you have done that)—you simply being you was healing. I don't think I am saying this very well, but this is what I will try and flesh out over the next few weeks.

So the poem this week that I hope aligns itself with the idea embedded in this metaphor comes from… you guessed it, Mary Oliver. This poem is called "The Orchard" and while it might not be apparent how it relates, there is a moment in the poem that makes me think of the metaphor. And it is simply this: We strive to become mature, accomplished, professional etc. and Mary suggests that, similar to the "ripeness of the apple," it is those things that are our "downfall." As a result, it is while we are on the way and not our arrival that is redemptive. Again, I don't think I am saying this very well, but there you have it.

Your boy, D

The Orchard
By Mary Oliver

I have dreamed
of accomplishment.
I have fed

ambition.
I have traded
nights of sleep

for a length of work.
Lo, and I have discovered
how soft bloom

turns to green fruit,
which turns to sweet fruit.
Lo, and I have discovered

all winds blow cold
at last,
and the leaves,

so pretty, so many,
vanish
in the great, black

packet of time,
in the great, black
packet of ambition,

and the ripeness
of the apple
is its downfall.

MISHPACHA REFLECTIONS
Jo's Bench
By Colin Phill, Friend

Sometimes a headstone is simply not enough. Sometimes a more tangible, functional, and accessible monument is needed to grieve, honor, and reflect.

For some of the most special and seismic individuals, this takes shape in the form of a memorial landmark of some kind. If a family has been blessed with someone whose life demands such a place, it can become a physical symbol of the power that life provided and an extension of the blessing they were to their communities.

There are countless families across the world able to trace generations of truly incredible individuals, who will never experience the confluence of catastrophic loss and remarkable communal support required to see one of these memorials come to fruition.

The Hillis family now has two—beautifully and tragically connected in ways well beyond the obvious.

In 1995, JD Hillis passed at the age of eight, with his best friend and cousin, 10-year-old Jordan by his side.

Shortly thereafter, the JD Hillis Memorial Court was installed at the Al Davies Boys and Girls Club in Tacoma, Washington, where it remains to this day.

In the days immediately following Jordan's passing, as we came to terms with the finality of his absence, I couldn't get my mind off the need for a similar place that we could frequent to feel connected to Jordan.

Identifying the specific destination for a memorial of some kind for Jordan was one of the few easy moments of those incredibly challenging weeks after his passing. Everyone is from somewhere. At its best, our relationship with our hometowns is eternal, formative, and symbiotic. Tacoma gave to Jordan what it could, although for someone with his depth, ambition, and curiosity, there were limits to what she could provide. These traits took Jordan all over the world, from New York to London to Norway to Sicily to Thailand and countless adventurous locales in between. That said, there was never any question as to where Jordan considered *home*.

His reach within this city is far and wide. From the halls of Mount Tahoma to the trails of the Five Mile Drive and every point in between, it'd be hard to find a stone in this city that Jordan left unturned. Among the myriad of specific landmarks throughout the city that I most closely associate with Jordan, without question Old Town Dock is where I personally have always felt nearest to him.

One of the many passions that I'm proud to have shared with Jordan is a magnetic pull to be near, on, or in saltwater whenever possible, particularly the cold, beautiful, and life-giving waters of the South Puget Sound. For us this desire often manifested itself in the form of plunges into Commencement Bay off Old Town Dock.

For nearly 20 years Jordan and I, alongside a select group of brave and willing participants, have welcomed each and every new year with a Polar Plunge on January 1st, even coining ourselves the "Old Town Polar Bear Society."

After instantaneous identification of Old Town Dock as the only viable venue, the dialogue then turned to what form this memorial would take. Those who knew Jordan best can confirm that sitting still was not his natural disposition. Thus, a bench may seem like an odd choice as a means to honor someone who would much rather be sprinting up and down the stairs of Stadium Bowl, untangling a fishing net in Bristol Bay, or running the Boston Marathon than relaxing on a bench. But in this case, our hope was that a bench would provide a symbolic extension of a place for Jordan to finally rest. His motor, passion, and drive were truly unmatched, and I have never felt the term more properly applied and deserving than when we all pray that Jordan "RESTS in peace."

The logistics of seeing this bench through to installation proved to be a welcomed and engaging bit of purposeful distraction throughout the grieving process. As are many (most) things when coordinating with a city or government institution, the process was certainly not as clean and expeditious as I originally and naively envisioned. On the other hand, the call to action and raising the funds to cover the donation necessary to see the bench installed could not have been more prompt. While I'd love to take credit in the successful crowdsourcing or position my small involvement in the process as anything other than clerical, the reality is that the overwhelming outpouring of support and generosity of so many was undoubtedly one of the most humbling and inspiring things I've ever been a part of. What I originally hoped could be a small, thankful, and symbolic gesture to a man and family that has already given me so much, ended up with me, yet again, benefiting from Jordan and his extraordinary community.

Beyond my selfish desire to have a place to go anytime I want to feel near Jordan, or to channel a bit of his tenacity, or to recalibrate using his compass, my primary ambition and hope for this bench was that it would become a beacon of sorts. A place where Jordan's village can forever visit, and often gather, to share stories, reflect on his values, and further build on his legacy via memories and new relationships.

On March 24th, 2024, countless members from all aspects of Jordan's community gathered on a gorgeous Sunday afternoon to dedicate and bless his bench. Walking down the dock towards his bench, seeing the throng of people spanning the width of Old Town Dock while Jordan's children Londyn and JD climbed on their father's bench was as powerful a visual as I've experienced.

Alongside Jordan's dad and two brothers, Father Steve Lantry and Pastor Tad Monroe prayed for the bench. They so beautifully and eloquently encapsulated so much of what I have tried to capture here regarding our hopes and ambitions of the future of this memorial.

Father Lantry shared some insights and additional context into the phrase that accompanies Jordan's name on the plaque on the back of the bench. *Miserando atque eligendo*, which is the papal motto of Pope Francis, and translates to "because he saw him through the eyes of mercy and chose him" or more simply, "having mercy, he called him."

After some additionally powerful and spirited words from those closest to Jordan, a subset of the mass was inspired enough to partake in one of Jo's favorite pastimes: the aforementioned Polar Plunge. There has always been something spiritual and cleansing about our jumps into Commencement Bay, but as we leapt off the dock doing our best renditions of a variety of iconic Jordan Hillis poses, dives, and quotes, the water felt cleansing and healing in a way that I've never experienced. That post-plunge endorphin rush was compounded that day by the hugs, laughs, and tears that were shared on and around that bench that afternoon and is a feeling I hope I can somehow recapture often.

Now while I wouldn't dare attempt to abridge the sentiments of my dear friends Father Lantry and Pastor Tad, one common theme that was shared by so many that day was that we all plan to frequent Jordan's bench, and in doing so, hope to find solace in being near him and on the most serendipitous of occasions, being near others who loved him as well.

See you there.

Jo,   MAY 27, 2011

So here we are: the last letter of May and the first one where, as I stated last week, I will attempt to try and articulate the things you have taught me while you have been in prison.

If someone came up to me on the street and asked me what it was that initially impacted me as a result of your crime and incarceration, I would answer that it was your acceptance of responsibility. This may appear less than heroic, but it surfaces from countless experiences I have had with others and from reflecting on my own pilgrimage as the almost universal quest to not take responsibility. In particular, there are three images of you accepting responsibility that I still meditate on that give me courage for my own life.

The first was when I saw you that first day in County. In the midst of some horrific realities ranging from being roughed up by the police to looking at some serious time to the conditions themselves, you were so quick to apologize and own your part. I think specifically of how you had put Ryan's goodwill and trust in jeopardy by using his place to deal drugs. Given how deep your friendship is, this must have caused you great angst which can often move people to figure out a way to justify themselves. You immediately took responsibility.

The second was watching you not be treated well in a variety of ways by the prison system. Things like no food, bad sleeping quarters, abuse by certain officials, and yet—at least to me— you never complained and even sort of hinted at the idea that this was what it meant to live with the ramification of what you did: another example to me of owning up to your responsibility.

The third one was the most difficult of all days when Whit and I came out to visit you on Ryan and Kasi's wedding day. We knew it was going to be tough, but on top of that you had just come from a miserable night of being out on the water with that crew you didn't get along with and they made you an hour late for your time with Whit and me. I don't think I have ever seen you in a more miserable state. But what was remarkable was the way that you constantly said you were sorry to Whit and I for the way you were feeling. It might seem like a small thing, but I walked away saying to myself, "*There* is someone who owns their shit."

Jo, there is so much more, but thank you for reminding me in some deep and abiding ways what it means to take responsibility.

The poem this week is one that I won't comment on because of space and time (in other words, I have already written too much), but I think you will like the way he describes the "inner dialogue" in all of us.

Much love, D

Self-Portrait
By Edward Hirsch

I lived between my heart and my head,
like a married couple who can't get along.

I lived between my left arm, which is swift
and sinister, and my right, which is righteous.

I lived between a laugh and a scowl,
and voted against myself, a two-party system.

My left leg dawdled or danced along,
my right cleaved to the straight and narrow.

My left shoulder was like a stripper on vacation,
my right stood upright as a Roman soldier.

Let's just say that my left side was the organ
donor and leave my private parts alone,

but as for my eyes, which are two shades
of brown, well, Dionysus, meet Apollo.

Look at Eve raising her left eyebrow
while Adam puts his right foot down.

No one expected it to survive,
but divorce seemed out of the question.

I suppose my left hand and my right hand
will be clasped over my chest in the coffin

and I'll be reconciled at last,
I'll be whole again.

SUMMER

Jordan,   JUNE 3, 2011

So sorry for the belatedness of this letter. My time got pushed this week with the group from Thailand in town, along with my board chair, and two of my colleagues. I should quickly add that it has been enjoyable to see Nit and it reminded me of the wonderful time we had together in Thailand. In fact, I was telling Nit (do you remember this) that she was the first person you and I met upon arriving in Bangkok. I will always remember driving into the city with you and encountering the smells, sounds, sensations, and the heat! Nit has asked if you are still as tall and good looking as she remembers you to be.

Well, here we are—two weeks and counting. In reflecting on the next lesson you taught me while you were in the joint, I was reminded of a poem that I am sending you this week by a guy named Charles Bukowski. I should add that I think you would enjoy him. He is very transparent and honest. I would almost go so far as to say he is "raw" in the sense that he does not seem very concerned with how you—the reader—might receive his words. This poem is called "Everywhere, Everywhere" and the reason that you made me think of it is the way I have watched you battle, struggle, confess, wonder, about the nature of your anger. From my estimation you have never denied its reality in your life and you have also never denied that it is the thing that has gotten you into some of your trouble.

His opening line—"amazing, the energy we burn fueling our anger. Amazing, how one moment we can be snarling a beast, then a few moments later, forgetting what or why"—seems to perfectly capture the way you have described how you feel on the inside. Do you concur? The reason I bring it up is that you have, through your reflection on your anger, helped me become more honest with certain feelings I have. Similar to you, I have an "anger" that burns within me. Unlike you, I have not been as honest. Thank you for that.

His next line, however, is even more convicting and again, a lesson that you have taught me. He begins to reflect on what anger does by writing, "lifetimes completely used up, given over to the pettiest rancor and hatred." Again, I know this has not been easy in your life, but I think of the many times I have sat with you and watched you honestly talk, while being angry, about how futile your anger is and also the ways it is destroying many of your friends. I have walked away from these times praying that I will be able to be this honest about some of the ways my life is being eaten up by some of these fights I am in with God, others, and myself.

Finally, and this is the most frightening line in the poem, Bukowski says that the final stage of anger is that it consumes who we are—our emotions, intellect, will, relationships—that when "death" shows up there will be "nothing left to take away." In effect, because of anger, we will already be walking dead men. You have confronted this fact, Jo. You have not yet come up with the answers you want, but you recognize that if anger continues to do its thing in you and others it will kill us all.

So, my brother, thanks for teaching me these very uncomfortable lessons about facing my own demons. I am a much better man because of you.

Your boy, D

Everywhere, Everywhere
By Charles Bukowski

amazing, the energy we burn
fueling our anger.
amazing, how one moment we can be
snarling like a beast, then
a few moments later,
forgetting what or
why.
not hours of this or days or
months or years of this
but decades,
lifetimes
completely used up,
given over to the pettiest
rancor and
hatred.
finally
there is nothing here for death to
take
away.

MISHPACHA REFLECTIONS
Mishpacha
By Melissa Monroe, Friend

I pen this as I sit on Jordan's memorial bench under a crystal clear PNW early summer sky, facing the cross beam from which he used to jump into the Sound—free—or at least that's how I'd like to imagine him.

Jordan Hillis was the personification of the sacred and the profane, like Simone Weil's two things awakening the soul—beauty and affliction[55]—come to life in one person. What a gift from the heavens, and, oh my god, was it startling. Like, in every way. Admirable and unnerving at the same time. I loved him for it, because it's what made Jordan spectacularly Jordan, but I hate it too because it is also why he is no longer with us, at least not in the way that I want. I know in my heart this is a consequence of the gift and burden of beauty and affliction.

Jordan gave me the gift of *mishpacha*—he embodied its value and lived it. *Mishpacha*, the Jewish term for *family*, which is so much more than the typical western notion or American version of a nuclear family. *Mishpacha* is who you choose to love, bring close, invite in. It's not bound by blood or marriage; it's free of that and anything that might seek to contain it. And Jordan was not one to be contained (again, something I both love and hate). *Mishpacha* is expansive and inclusive and has the effect of making one bigger in soul. And Jordan, dear soul, was real fucking big.

---

55 Simone Weil, *Simone Weil, an Anthology*, ed. Siân Miles (New York: Grove Press, 2000), 82.

Jordan made me part of his mishpacha. He loved me, brought me close, celebrated me, and unfailingly included me. No secondhand invitations with Jordan. He reached out directly, looked me in the face, and said, 'I want you there,' and I knew he meant it. He wouldn't say it if he didn't. Whether it was a birthday party or celebrating a return from fishing or some other festive gathering, he extended an invitation. Even when he was vulnerable, Jordan trusted and risked. He defended and protected fiercely all those he loved. Always, unfailingly.

Mishpacha is a rarity in our neck of the woods. Too often it goes unnoticed or underappreciated. It entirely escapes some people's imaginations of what life and family and community could be. But this is true: *Mishpacha* saved my life. It might be the single greatest gift I've ever received. God incarnate. A bit of heaven on earth. And Jordan gave it to me.

Jordan,   JUNE 10, 2011

Yikes... after this letter I will have one last one to write. It is still somewhat hard for me to believe.

By way of describing to you the next lesson you taught me, I wanted to recap that first two. If you remember, two weeks ago I said the lesson that you have taught me over the past 20 months has been your capacity to accept responsibility for your actions. The one that I wrote about last week is your courage in confronting those darker places in your life—particularly anger.

The third lesson you have taught me, which will be the gist of this letter, is your dance with mercy. Now this might seem a bit strange to you, but let me explain. I am very aware of how difficult this concept is for all of us. Primarily because I think we all long for it at some deep level and yet have to confront a world that seems so merciless in its very existence. If I was to summarize the tension it would be in the conversation you and I had in the car the day I took you out to work. Do you remember? We were talking about mercy and in effect you said, "Great idea, but it doesn't work on the street." I have continued to think long and hard about your comment and still don't fully know all of what I think, but my point in this letter is that you are willing to wrestle with this question at a profound level. A great example of this is *Les Miserables*. Don't you sense that the whole book in many ways is the tension between Valjean's view of life, which believes in mercy, and Javert whose whole goal was, as Hugo states, "not to be humane, not to be great, not to be sublime; it was to be irreproachable,"[56] which I interpret as a man without mercy? I, of course, will be very interested in what you make of my interpretation, but more important is that I have been blessed as I have watched you struggle with this issue. It seems to me that, bottom line, you want to believe in mercy, but if it's true it will have to be true on its own merits. In effect, either it is mercy or it is not. As Hugo himself says in the book, "Love has no middle term; either it destroys, or it saves."[57] That's you in a nutshell, Jo, and I am ever so thankful for the way you continue to teach what this means.

As a result of "this sermon" my poem this week is from Mary. It is called "Mysteries, Yes" and in my mind captures a bit of what I just tried to describe—specifically (and the reason I thought about this poem in light of you) her description of the two kinds of people. Her twin admonitions to "keep my distance, always from those who think they have the answers" and then encourages a person to keep the company of "those who say 'Look!' and laugh with astonishment, and bow their heads." Jo, you are one of those people for me whose company I want to keep because you help me "bow my head."

Your boy, D

---

56 Victor Hugo, *Les Miserables: The Only Complete and Unabridged Paperback Edition*, trans. Lee Fahnestock, Norman MacAfee, and Charles E. Wilbour (New York: Signet Classic, 1987), 1324.
57 Hugo, *Les Miserables*, 1004.

Mysteries, Yes
By Mary Oliver

Truly, we live with mysteries too marvelous
    to be understood.

How grass can be nourishing in the
    mouths of the lambs.
How rivers and stones are forever
    in allegiance with gravity
        while we ourselves dream of rising.
How two hands touch and the bonds will
    never be broken.
How people come, from delight or the
    scars of damage,
to the comfort of a poem.

Let me keep my distance, always, from those
    who think they have the answers.

Let me keep company always with those who say
    "Look!" and laugh in astonishment,
    and bow their heads.

Jordan,   JUNE 17, 2011

I never thought the day would come where I would be writing my last letter to you at the end of your process with Pierce County Jail, Shelton, McNeil Island, and now the Progress House. To give you a bit of a summary, I have written (counting this one) 62 letters and sent you 60 poems/articles/stories. The letter writing began April 9, 2010 and will officially end today, June 17, 2011. During this time you and I have reflected on a number of different topics ranging from forgiveness, mercy, the nature of strength, identity, loneliness, just to name a few. It has been a great joy for me and something that I have looked forward to every Friday morning. In truth, I am going to miss writing you and it seems to me that this issue—why I am going to miss writing you—is what this final letter should be about. And of course it corresponds with the poem I am sending you as well.

The poem—"Things I Didn't Know I Loved" by Mara Faulkner—is based on a guy who spent 13 years in prison. During his time in prison he began to reflect and discovered that there were a variety of things he did not know he loved until he did not have them. Mara's poem picks up on that theme. Similarly, my letter is a reflection to you on things I didn't know I loved until I had the chance each Friday to think and write to you.

I didn't know how much my heartache for your situation could be a heart that aches for you. I didn't know how deeply I admire your resolve until it was put to the test in such dreadful conditions. I did not know how much I love your keen mind and its hunger to read. I did not know how much I honor your clear sense of boundaries and the way you interfaced with cellmates and guards. I did not know how much I love your physical discipline and your willingness to run with less than adequate gear in the snow. I didn't know how much I love the way you and your brothers love each other in the midst of separation. I didn't know how much I appreciate you as a conversationalist and your forthright and candid reflections on life. I did not know how much a number—320741—could impact me and could be transformed from something that horrified me to something I am proud of because of the way you carried it. I did not know how much I love the way you wrestle with God and your quiet, firm, and important decision to say 'yes' to God's forgiveness. Finally, I did not know how much I love you and how very glad I am—regardless of circumstances—to be able to call you my son, my colleague, and my friend.

Thanks for all, Jo. It has been a great gift.

Your boy, D

Things I Didn't Know I Loved[58]
By Mara Faulkner

I know all this has been said a thousand times before and will be said after me.

-Nazim Hikmet, writing in exile after 13 years in prison

I didn't know I loved

the wrangle of phones and human voices, rough, insistent

until I entered this silence and closed the door.
I didn't know I loved

this silence until the hooked voices reached for me.
I didn't know I loved

didn't really know I loved the treeless prairies until green bars grew up

between my eyes, the airy sunset, and the moon.
Didn't know I loved

the thorny green thickets of my self

contrary and bear-haunted, until I took the straight smooth road

and found it strewn with death. I didn't know I loved

black bears lumbering through my dream toward my sister

whom I didn't know I loved

even though I've lost her now in the blind thicket and she

doesn't love me any more. I didn't know I loved

---

58 Mara Faulkner, "Things I Didn't Know I Loved," *America: The Jesuit Review*, June 6, 2011, https://www.americamagazine.org/issue/779/poem/things-i-didnt-know-i-loved

my mother until her rose-heart burst and bled
red petals into her chest, didn't know I loved
the garden of her flesh. And you, my God
under her ashes so silent and cold, I didn't know I loved
you until you woke every morning in my little stove
so lowly in your prison house of wood and flesh and fire
so eager and so needful of my hands. I didn't know I loved
my hands—clumsy, tender—until they stirred the fire

and found these words.

Conclusion: The Two Memorials

This memoir, while recalling the various events, encounters, and engagements of Jordan's life, is really a memoir about the anatomy of relationships. It was written with the recognition that the precious "I" that we so confidently cling to, is actually a "we." That in truth my and your "I" is constituted and woven together by our imitation of others. This imitative capacity that is in us, which can also be described as mimetic, can be used for good or ill. I believe it was this idea that Dr. King articulated so beautifully in his 1967 Christmas sermon on peace:

> *In a real sense all life is interrelated. All men are caught in an inescapable network of mutuality, tied in a single garment of destiny. Whatever affects one directly affects all indirectly. I can never be what I ought to be until you are what you ought to be, and you can never be what you ought to be until I am what I ought to be… This is the interrelated structure of reality.*[59]

The primary throughline in this memoir has been trying to tease out the implications of the "inescapable network" that King references, this anatomy of relationships that was mentioned above. The essays shared by friends and family unveiled a sense of how their "I's" were in fact a "we," and how this continues to sit at the heart of this village that lost Jordan. Father Steve Lantry, S.J. elegantly delivered the homily/eulogy at Jordan's Memorial Mass a month after he died stating "that

---

59 Martin L. King, 2011. "A Christmas Sermon on Peace." in *The Trumpet of Conscience* (N.p.: Beacon Press, 2011).

to know Jordan Hillis was a complicated grace." And if there was a model that embodied the "inescapable network" of this "complicated grace" it is the friendship of Joshua Dean (JD) Hillis and Jordan Michael Hillis and the two memorials in Tacoma that represent the lives they lived.

As noted by my brother Mark in his reflection, Jordan and JD were separated by 19 months and were best buddies. Most best buddies are characterized by their similarities. Jordan and JD were characterized by their differences. Jordan—blond, blue-eyed, and round, saw life as an exquisite challenge where no roof was too tall to climb, games were arenas to battle and decide who wins and who loses, and teachers' directions were in fact suggestions. You could take them or leave them. Jordan was Freud's id—instinctual, primal, aggressive. JD—brunette, hazel-eyed, and thin, thought you shouldn't go up on the roof in the first place, games were meant to meet people, and that teachers were right and should be obeyed. JD was Freud's ego—rational, reasonable, sane. They, from two different planets, became each other's muse. Because of each other they became better, broader, and bigger. And they are dead. A complicated grace.

When Jordan was 10, JD Hillis died on March 13th, 1995, of arteriovenous malformation (AVM) in my backyard.

In the aftermath, much of which can still not be fully remembered, or maybe more precisely, won't be remembered, we as family and friends gathered around the crushing solemnity of a funeral for a little boy who died too young. Amid the tears and the anguish, the question surfaced: How, if at all, do we honor this gracious little boy? The adults, in their adjudicated and risk-free way, suggested planting a cherry tree at the local church that would remind all of us how life keeps going on—a response that if it was heeded would have required the prerequisite investment of running down to the local nursery, picking out a tree, and paying the $50 dollar price tag. While considering this option, another suggestion surfaced.

"I think JD would think a tree sucked," declared Jordan in his uniquely low voice for someone so young. Over time, we would slowly and agonizingly begin to discover just how much the death of his beloved best friend would haunt 10-year old Jordan for the rest of his life. Jordan went further: "If we really wanted to do something for JD that he would like, we would help the place that he hoped he could play at some day—Al Davies Boys and Girls Club." When I asked what he had in mind, Jordan said, "The basketball court at Al Davies sucks (a favorite word of Jordan's when he was 10), and we should build a new one and name it after him." Jordan was referring to the gym where he and his two older brothers spent all their spare time. Sure enough, he was correct in his assessment of the condition of the court. Like many inner-city gyms, the Al Davies court was an amalgamation of old, chipped linoleum tile that, if you were slightly unaware while you were dribbling the basketball down the court, the ball had a likely chance of flying off in some unintended direction because the court was in such poor shape. When we tried to explain how expensive an endeavor like this might be, Jordan responded by simply saying, "Well, all I am saying is that if you want to do something for JD, he would have wanted a court." The drive for JD's Memorial Court was born.

Four months and $110,000 later, we dedicated the brand new maple wood court, six brand new baskets and back boards, and a new clock to the memory of JD. It now sits proudly in the heart of the Hilltop neighborhood of Tacoma as the JD Hillis Memorial Court, where every year at Christmas a tournament is held in his honor—along with the games of a countless number of young kids who play there every other day of the year. This memorial exists 29 years later because of Jordan's love for his cousin, JD. Ironically, it also exists in the very streets that would ultimately be a piece in the puzzle that led to Jordan's death. A complicated grace.

On September 7th, 2023, when JD would have been 36, Jordan, at 38, died in my arms in a parking lot of a drug overdose.

JD and Jo's deaths were vastly different: one plucked like an elegant orchid—beautiful, benign, beatific; the other, more briar-like in the end—wrecked, wracked, wrenched. Yet the village that was shaped by JD's death and celebrated him arose once again to celebrate Jordan. A complicated grace.

And Jordan's memorial? It took shape over the month-long wake that occurred between Jordan's death and his Memorial Mass on October 7th. In the course of conversations that always consisted of the retelling of some immortal tale, breaking of bread, and cups being supped, the idea of memorializing Jordan in the same way JD was, began to emerge.

The first was prosaic: to establish a college fund for his two beloved children, Jimmy David (the second JD) and Londyn. The village came together over the course of that month before the memorial and raised over $60,000 for their futures. It was a beautiful gesture giving his two children a leg up into the future.

The second was poetic: to dedicate a bench on Jordan's beloved Tacoma waterfront on the Old Town Dock. Supported by the wonderful leadership of Colin Phill (who in his reflection provides you with the nuts, bolts, and underpinnings of how it came together) the bench became a reality. The village came together and raised $6,200 for the bench to be placed where people of any type, size, shape, color, orientation—Jordan's people—will be able to sit and experience peace that largely eluded Jordan all his life. And the plaque they will lean against? The Latin phrase from St. Matthew 9:13 (also Pope Francis's motto) used by Father Steve Lantry in his eulogy/homily at Jordan's Memorial Mass: *miserando atque eligendo*, which can be translated 'having mercy, he called him.' A complicated grace.

One might ask, 'Really? Two memorials for the same family, between best friends, in the same city?' Unusual? Odd? Cruel? Circumspect? Or is it simply what life serves up—that "his sun rises on the evil and on the good" and sends "rain on the just and on the unjust"—and that what really matters is how the village—the mishpacha—decides to carry their grief. Does the village detach and begin the sad, slow, saunter toward isolation and introspection or run headlong into connection leading to communion that can bring about the faint outlines of hope? I perceive, however faintly, that Carl Jung had the answer to these questions that are restlessly ricocheting in my head when he stated that healing was not so much a matter of solving our problems, but rather growing larger than them.[60] I sense this is at play, for which I am forever grateful.

There is a scene from one of Jordan's favorite films, *Equalizer 2*, that captures this reality perfectly and was the last text I ever sent him. The protagonist, Robert McCall, played by Denzel Washington, confronts a father who has kidnapped his daughter from the estranged wife he systematically abused and taken her to Turkey. On a train, having dispatched the henchmen, Robert confronts his antagonist and says, "There are two kinds of pain in this world. The pain that hurts, the pain that alters. Today, you get to choose."[61] This is the choice that every village faces as they encounter loss. *A Complicated Grace* is the story of one village's choice in hopes that we will be altered.

---

60 C. G. Jung, "Alchemical Studies," *Collected Works of C. G. Jung*. Vol. 13. (Princeton, New Jersey: Princeton University Press, 1983), 18.
61 Anthony Fuqua, dir. *Equalizer 2*. United States: Sony Pictures, 2018.

Postscript

The phone call from my son Patrick came amid a very dark moment. I was continuing to try (not very successfully) and come to grips with Jordan's passing on top of a two-year stretch that included other deaths: a job change, the passing of my father and brother in-laws, the loss of two very close friends, and a six-week stint of jury duty on a double homicide case where a grandson killed his grandparents. I had received a diagnosis from my therapist for PTSD and was being treated as such but feeling a deep desire to withdraw and isolate. When Patrick invited me to join him and two of my grandchildren, 10-year-old Myles and seven-year-old Fiona, along with their dog Boomer for a four-hour road trip to a soccer tournament in a part of the state of Washington that is physically very unappealing, everything in me wanted to say, "Thanks, but no thanks." But in the end, I said yes, and I am deeply thankful that I did.

On the morning of the soccer tournament Patrick and Myles were watching a premier soccer league game and cheering on their favorite team, Arsenal. I was in a corner reading a book and Fiona, being Fiona, was playing by herself. At some point Fiona (who I call Fi) came up to me and said, "Grandpa D, I can see that you're not really into all this soccer stuff. How about you and I go on a walk down by the river?" I quickly accepted the invitation and headed down to the riverfront of the mighty Columbia.

As we walked, I asked Fi what the plan was and she replied, "I am going to take you on a meditative tour." I chuckled and asked what this consisted of. She replied by saying, "Well, do you see all of the benches?" There were about 12 of them. "We are going to sit on each one for a minute and then compare and contrast them with Uncle Jo's bench. And don't worry Grandpa D, I will keep time and keep us moving."

Before we even started, Fi ran down a hill into a briar patch to pick up some trash. She quickly proclaimed that she wanted to save the environment and that it would be hard for her to meditate if she knew there was trash out there like that and she didn't do anything about it. I began to sense something was afoot.

And so off we went. We got to the first bench, and I watched with great pride how my little granddaughter settled into a cross-legged yoga lotus pose, lifted up her hands, and quieted herself. I followed suit, closed my eyes, lifted my hands, and tried to quiet myself. A few seconds later I heard Fi say, "Okay Grandpa D, time to go to the next bench."

Two benches later we again began the routine of closed eyes, lifted hands, quieted self, when I heard Fi say, "You know Grandpa D, sometimes I find my meditative experiences are helped when I keep my eyes open." As I slowly opened my eyes, I saw my granddaughter staring out at the Columbia. She went on. "For example, do you see the way the wind is gliding across the river and making little waves? Doesn't it remind you of God's Spirit? You wouldn't have noticed that if your eyes were closed, right?" I responded that that did make sense while also noticing a growing sense inside of me that we had entered a space that felt increasingly sacred. She went further and said,

"Do you see the leaves, the pine needles and all the other plants and all the different colors of green being used? I mean, c'mon Grandpa D, that is remarkable!"

At this point I had entered into what I sensed was a liminal space—to be on the precipice of something new but not quite there yet—and that I needed to follow her lead.

She then said, "And look over there, Grandpa D. Do you see the wall?" What she was pointing at was a granite wall made up of six slabs of granite, probably six feet high and four feet wide. I told Fi I did, and she proceeded to say, "And do you see that two of the slabs have fallen down?" Again, I responded in the affirmative. She grabbed my hand as we sat on the bench and said, "That's you and me, Grandpa D. We have had a tough year. But we're going to get back up."

And with that, Fiona promenaded off to the next bench while I sat in stunned silence, trying to come to grips with what just happened, and knowing without a shadow of a doubt that young Fi, representing the village, the mishpacha, looked into my complicated life and found a grace. A complicated grace to be sure, but a grace nonetheless.

Acknowledgements

Over the course of working on this memoir, the title—*A Complicated Grace*—has lived up to its billing. Many have been the days that felt desperately dark with little to no light and then, often in miraculously mysterious and merciful ways, a shiny sliver—a smell, a memory, a text, a conversation—would appear seemingly out of nowhere. One of those slivers of light shone as I was reading the noted Catholic theologian, Hans Urs Von Balthasar, who is a favorite of mine. He jotted the following that captured in two exquisite sentences what became a lifeline for me as I continue to process Jordan's death: "He (Christ) alone would henceforth be the measure and thus also the meaning of all importance. He wanted to sink so low that in the future all falling would be a falling into him, and every streamlet of bitterness and despair would henceforth run down into his lowermost abyss."[62] It seemed to me at the time that Von Balthasar was illuminating the deeply scandalous truth of what Psalm 139 makes so wonderfully clear, "If I say, 'Surely the darkness shall fall on me,' Even the night shall be light about me; Indeed, the darkness shall not hide from You, But the night shines as the day; The darkness and the light are both alike to *You*."[63]

Could it be true? That "falling" and "darkness" are actually our path forward to light? A Complicated Grace indeed!

One of the things that I am carrying forward as I consider that this memoir fell repeatedly into Von Balthasar's "every streamlet

---

62 Hans Urs von Balthasar, *Heart of the World* (San Francisco: Ignatius Press, 1979), 43.
63 Psalm 139:11-12, NKJV

of bitterness and despair" and the Psalmist's sense of darkness falling on me, is the reality of "falling into" community—family, friends, colleagues, sisters and brothers, and every other kind of possible support that was humanly possible. As opposed to trying to lift me up in a muscular and (albeit well-intended) rehabilitative way, they instead got beneath me and provided soft places for me to land time and time again. And while to list all would become a memoir in and of itself, there are a few that provided a particularly soft place for me to fall that, without their contribution, this volume would never have seen the light of day.

The embryonic moment of this volume came from Michael "Burk" Burke. Burk, who in many ways is a brother to Patrick, Ryan, and Jordan, was just getting out of prison when Jordan was going in. I asked Burk to provide a "graduate seminar" to our family regarding the dos and don'ts in relationship to an incarcerated family member. I distinctly remember two things. The first was advising us to avoid any mention of missing Jordan when it came to holidays, birthdays, and special occasions, as all this would do is remind Jordan of what he is missing out on. The second was to flood Jordan's mailbox with mail; this is manna from heaven for those inside the joint. It was from this directive by Burk that I was nudged to write Jordan every Friday where, because of our mutual love of poetry (Jordan was the poet laureate of his high school), I would pick a poem and send a brief note of commentary on how it might be helpful to the two of us. The poems and letters that are the throughline of this memoir are because of Burk, his seminar and the pastoral path it provided for me to love my son and a soft place to fall.

However, it should be noted that the letters and poems were

never meant to see the light of day if not for Father Steve Lantry. They were simply a conversation between a son and his father living through and in a desperate space. It was Steve in his eulogy/homily at Jordan's Memorial Mass that used the phrase "to know Jordan Hillis was a complicated grace" that stirred my imagination and set in motion the possibility of this book. The phrase was so faithful, fierce, and fecund in its description and memory of Jordan that it is as though this memoir demanded to be written. Steve's poetic and psychological insight gave me a soft place to fall.

As important as Michael's and Steve's contributions were (and this cannot be overstated) *A Complicated Grace* would not exist without Kate Schmidgall, Obiekwe (Obi) Okolo, Avery Marks, and the BitterSweet Creative team. This is our second dance together, our first being the *City As Playground* anthology. I use the word "dance" intentionally regarding BitterSweet Creative because one of the descriptions of the Holy Spirit and her activity in scripture is that of "divine choreography"—a cosmic dance taking place between people that is orchestrated by the Holy Spirit herself. There was a particular dance step that especially touched me: Obi's willingness to allow my oldest granddaughter, Kenedee (KD) Ryan Hillis, to have a role in the design of the book. Thank you, Obi, for that gift and thank you, KD, for your wonderful contribution. This was one small example of BitterSweet's repeated demonstrations of deftness of touch, sensitivity to voice, and nuanced sightline that exhibits the reality that the Holy Spirit is always dancing with us. BitterSweet has provided me with the courage and confidence for this project and another important and soft place for me to fall.

And then there are the contributors: To Patrick and Ryan Hillis (which also includes the incredible support of their partners Teresa Bethany and Kasi) whose brotherhood with Jordan is beauty beyond description: General MacArthur's last line in his *A Father's Prayer*, "And then I will dare to whisper I have not lived in vain" is more true than it has ever been. To Uncles Mark and Mike Hillis (with the prayerful commitment of their spouses Cheryl and Kathy), and Cousin Tyler (representing Hillis cousins: JD, Cory, Chase, Matthew, and Whitney; spouses Alia, Olivia, and Taylor, and children Jayde, Luisa, and Finley): Because of your modeling, Jordan deeply believed what J.R.R. Tolkien wrote, "The world is indeed full of peril, and in it there are many dark places; but still there is much that is fair, and though in all lands love is now mingled with grief, it grows perhaps the greater."[64] To Keilah Fanene, Steve Lantry, Colin McArthur, Melissa Monroe, Tad Monroe, Dave Osterhaus, Colin Phill, Lana Rocke, Todd Silver, Lina Thompson, and Cornelius Williams: What can be said? Your commitment to Jordan, exemplified by your gracious reflections, provided a whole new layer to the Hebrew word, *mishpacha*. As Shakespeare stated so elegantly and I have used repeatedly, "I can no other answer make but thanks, and thanks, and ever thanks."[65] Countless times you waited at the bottom as I tumbled over, and gave me a soft place to fall.

As a result of some very good fortune and some very good friends, I have been provided with some very good help. For the past

---

64 John Ronald R. Tolkien, *The Fellowship of the Ring: Being the First Part of the Lord of the Rings* (N.p.: HarperCollins, 2020).

65 William Shakespeare, J. C Smith, and Ernest Hunter Wright, *As You Like It* (Boston, New York etc. D.C. Heath & Co, 1916) Pdf. https://www.loc.gov/item/16020493/

seven months I have sat with Charlotte Malkmus, a therapist of remarkable dexterity. She is fluent in not only the hard science of how we are wired but understands and operationalizes the soft art of presence. It is hard for me to overstate my sense of indebtedness to her. This memoir would not have been possible if she had not helped me unlock some doors and windows to my soul. She waited for me at the bottom as I repeatedly fell.

To Jordan's dudes, Nash Welch and Jeremiah "Hurt" Larkin, Blue Money: Impossible to exaggerate what you meant to Jordan and what you mean to the larger Hillis family. There is a line from the film beloved by the three of you, *300*, that distills the essence of your relationship. Stelios states to King Leonidas in their last battle, "It's an honor to die at your side." Leonidas responds by saying, "It's an honor to have lived at yours."[66] I think the following would be a good translation, where the two of you would have said, if given the opportunity, "It's an honor to have lived at your side, Jordan." And Jordan would have said to the two of you, "It is an honor to have died at yours." Thank you for the many memories that provided me and the Hillis family with soft places to fall.

To Sara Erickson Melchior with some gracious assistance from Kerri Feider, Jonathan Hayden and the aforementioned Melissa Monroe: When Kate said yes to the project, I had a moment of panic as I was the proverbial dog that caught the bumper. I needed someone to step in and be the "point guard" on this project, and Sara immediately came to mind. The poet

---

66 Zach Snyder, dir. *300*. CA: Warner Brothers, 2007.

William Blake wrote, "Execution is the chariot of genius,"[67] and execution she provided, through communication, liaisoning, and assisting and providing me with wise counsel. Sara, Kerri, Jonathan, and Melissa were the support I needed, as well as consistently a soft place I fell to time and again.

To the "generations" whose shoulders we stand on: Jordan's grandparents Patrick Donlan Coogan who preceded him in death, Patty "Gigi" Coogan, and Carolyn "Nana" Hillis. Time and again you provide a place and presence into which I could fall.

The Coogans: Steve with Nancy, Sean and Nick, Tim who has passed and his widow Franca, Tom, Peter and Katy, John with Sam and Maddie. As I write this I am mindful of the grief and pain that has been particularly present for all of you these past two years with the passing of beloved Patrick Donlan and Timothy Patrick, which now includes Jordan Michael. St. Teresa of Avila captured my sense of your journey well where she wrote, "It shouldn't be thought that he/she who suffers isn't praying, for he/she is offering this to God."[68] Thank you for taking the time to share in this suffering as we have fallen into prayer together.

And finally, but by no means lastly, to Jordan's mother and my wife, Teresa Marie Elizabeth Coogan Hillis, Mimi to the grands and the "Little Flower" to others. It was you that gave the official okay to take on this difficult task of reflecting on what it means to lose a child and talk about the successes and failures woven throughout this journey. Your courage in allowing me

---

67 Edwin J. Ellis, *The Real Blake: A Portrait Biography* (N.p.: FB&C Limited, 2015), 378.
68 Kieran, Kavanaugh, trans. *The Collected Letters of St. Teresa of Avila: 1546-1577* (Washington D.C.: ICS Publications, 2001), 369.

to chase this down is magnanimous and maternal, although it might not feel like it right now. Most parents' first instinct would be to hide or protect, but you inspired and liberated me and many other voices to lovingly and honestly reflect on your baby. You ran toward this reality, thereby providing the impulse for the memoir. You and I fell together, and I thank you for the ways we provided each other with a soft place to fall.

And to you, Jordan Michael Hillis. On countless occasions during your time on earth you chose a "pain that alters" and that too offered me a soft place to fall. Thank you, broheim.

About the Author

Dave Hillis is a father to three adult sons, Patrick, Ryan, and Jordan (who passed away in September, 2023). He and his wife Teresa have resided in Tacoma, Washington for over 40 years, raising their family as they worked for the spiritual and social renewal of Tacoma as well as other cities around the world.

He currently serves as the Samuel Shoemaker Senior Innovation Fellow with the Leadership Foundations (LF) Colangelo Carpenter Innovation Center, devoting himself to thinking, writing, and speaking about the idea and ramifications of seeing our cities as God's playgrounds. Dave's perspective was honed as an area and regional director of urban Young Life, president of the Northwest Leadership Foundation, and president of the global network of Leadership Foundations. He received his undergraduate degree from Western Washington University, his Master of Divinity from Fuller Theological Seminary, and his Doctor of Ministry from Bakke Graduate University. Dave has served as an adjunct professor and is a guest lecturer and teacher at various urban ministry and leadership conferences. He has served on the boards of numerous community organizations and is deeply committed to his Catholic parish, St. Leo. Dave authored *Cities: Playgrounds or Battlegrounds?*, which tells the history and impact of the LF Global Network, and was a contributor and editor of the anthology, *City As Playground*, a collection of 19 essays and interviews from academicians and practitioners.

In his spare time, he is an avid reader of poetry and an aficionado of all things cigars and scotch.